Motorbooks International

MIL-TECH SERIES

NORTHROP B-2
STEALTH BOMBER

The Complete History, Technology, and Operational Development of the Stealth Bomber

Bill Sweetman

First published in 1992 by Motorbooks International Publishers & Wholesalers, PO Box 2, 729 Prospect Avenue, Osceola, WI 54020 USA

Motorbooks International books are also available at discounts in bulk quantity for industrial or sales-promotional use. For details write to Special Sales Manager at the Publisher's address

Library of Congress Cataloging-in-Publication Data
Sweetman, Bill.
  Northrop B-2 Stealth Bomber / Bill
  Sweetman.
    p. cm.
  Includes index.
  ISBN 0-87938-599-5
  1. B-2 bomber. I. Title.
UG1242.B6S943 1992
358.4'282—dc20   92-4353

On the front cover: The Northrop B-2 Stealth Bomber lifts off the runway at Air Force Plant 42 at Palmdale, California, on its first test flight. *John Andrews Collection via James C. Goodall*

On the back cover: Top, this diagram shows how the B-2 evolved from its original wing design (left) to the production configuration. *Northrop*. Bottom, four B-2s in final assembly at Palmdale. *Northrop*

Printed and bound in the United States of America

Contents

Introduction

Of Bombers, Quotes, and Votes

A lie can be half-way around the world before the truth has got its boots on.

—Mark Twain

Show trials and witch hunts are parodies of legal ritual—where the prosecutor is also the judge, where the defense speaks only as the prosecutor permits, and where evidence is presented or withheld at the prosecutor's unchallenged whim.

If you thought we buried the show trial with Joe Stalin and Joe McCarthy, think again. On February 18, 1990, CBS television aired a *60 Minutes* segment on the B-2. Billed as journalism, it was a classic example of a show trial.

The story was demonstrably unbalanced. Five of the six people interviewed by Mike Wallace were on-the-record opponents of the B-2. The other was retired Adm. William Crowe, former chairman of the Joint Chiefs of Staff, whose comments were given less air time than those of any of the five B-2 opponents.

One of the anti-B-2 witnesses was Michael Brower, of the Union of Concerned Scientists (UCS). *60 Minutes* did not inform its viewers that the UCS is a lobby group that has opposed every nuclear modernization program since the eighties.

Also appearing for the prosecution, Representative Mike Synar of Oklahoma voiced concern that the B-2 might draw funds from other aircraft that might be needed in the nineties. The B-2 was one of four big new warplane projects facing a review at that time; one of the others was the A-12 attack plane (later canceled) being built in Tulsa, Oklahoma. This fact was not mentioned.

What *60 Minutes* did not say about Synar and Brower was in accordance with the rules of a show trial: the prosecutor decides what evidence shall or shall not be presented to the jury.

Defense analysts Chuck Myers and Thomas Amlie also took part in the show. They said that the B-2 was not invisible. Nobody has ever claimed that it is, literally; Stealth makes things difficult, not impossible, to detect.

Myers and Amlie said that older, long-wavelength, low-frequency radars can detect some stealthy targets better than newer, high-frequency radars. That has been public knowledge for years—as has been the fact that low-frequency radars are big and clumsy, hampered by interference from other radio traffic, and not very accurate. That is why newer radars operate at higher frequencies.

Neither Amlie nor Myers was asked about the limitations or disadvantages of low-frequency radars because, in a

4

show trial, the prosecutor decides which questions are asked and which are not.

The other witness was freelance writer Michael Dennis. *60 Minutes* claimed that "new information," obtained by Dennis, showed that the B-2 program would cost $110 billion to $120 billion, not $70 billion as the US Air Force (USAF) had told Congress. "And what you're saying is that Congress was being lied to by the Air Force to the tune of $40 to $50 billion dollars?" asked Wallace. "I believe that's correct," responded Dennis.

Not one shred of evidence was presented to support this allegation of criminal misconduct and none has appeared since. The General Accounting Office—no friend of the USAF—found no sign of such an overrun in its report on the B-2, issued a few days later. But Dennis' statement went unchallenged on the air; in a show trial, the defense is not permitted to examine witnesses.

If the *60 Minutes* piece had been an aberration, it might not merit such an autopsy. But it is merely an egregious example of the blend of ignorance and petulant malice shown by too many reporters and politicians in their approach to the B-2 controversy.

A detailed study of TV coverage of the B-2 program was conducted for the Aerospace Education Foundation (an affiliate of the Air Force Association). The bomber was rarely mentioned on network news between its roll-out and first flight tests—unless the media could quote critics of the B-2 or rehash its technical or political problems.

The print media do better sometimes, but not always. In the fall of 1990, I spent most of an hour talking to one reporter, who wanted to know why the USAF didn't want to stage a public test of a B-2 against an FAA surveillance radar. I explained that a single test against an uncalibrated radar would be meaningless, producing (at great expense) no data that would be of any technical or tactical use. The reporter said that he understood.

In his article, he quoted a former Pentagon official as saying much the same thing, in more technical language. Instead of attempting a paraphrase, the reporter cutely rendered it incomprehensible to the general reader and implied that the B-2 managers had no good reason for avoiding such a test.

B-2 costs are usually exaggerated in the media. Sometimes, the exaggeration is blatant, such as the *Washington Monthly* article that stated, "In 1981, the Air Force estimated that a force of 133 B-2s could be procured for $32.7 billion. By mid-1989, the cost had grown to $70.2 billion." But the first total was in 1981 dollars, while the second included inflation beyond the year 2000. The distinction is so basic to the economics of defense that it is hard to attribute such an oversight to mere sloppiness or innumeracy.

The *60 Minutes* segment and the *Washington Monthly* article raise another general question, If the B-2 is such a bad idea, why is it apparently impossible to make a compelling case against it without distorting the facts?

The B-2 is usually described as costing $865 million each, even though this number misleads much more than it informs. Reporters invariably say that it is the most readily comprehensible number available and that their readers cannot understand complex accounting. But try this (accurate as of September 1991): "The US Air Force wants to buy seventy-five B-2s at a cost of $64.8 billion, of which some $31 billion has already been spent on research and development. B-2 opponents want to stop after fifteen aircraft, saving about $30 billion over the next ten years." Is that any more complicated than the American League standings?

In a June 1990 media briefing at Palmdale, the Air Force described the B-2 and its planned missions in unprecedented detail. One reporter for a major national newspaper summed up the USAF's entire case for the B-2 in one word: "tendentious." In the same report, he quoted Representative John Kasich as saying that the B-2 would "bankrupt America." Considering that the program's peak annual cost is one per cent of the defense budget, or roughly equivalent to what American citizens spend each year on bouncing checks, Kasich's statement could (and should) have been called something more than tendentious.

In September 1991, it was revealed that one of the B-2's Stealth tests had not produced the predicted reduction in reflectivity. Washington panicked. Most mass media reports on the problem missed a basic and critical point: that radar cross-section is dependent on radar frequency and aspect. Stealth is not a single parameter, like weight. Without that basic (and well-known) fact, it was impossible for readers to put the story into perspective, and the media failed to do so.

Why worry about the media? The media's view of the B-2 shapes the political debate, and not the other way around. Even if members of Congress were all geniuses, they could not possibly stay on top of all the issues on which Congress votes every day. They rely for their detailed information on their staffers.

It would be nice to think that these staffers were all experts. They aren't. Many of them are political wannabees just out of college in the home state, and whence do they get their information? That's right, the newspapers and the TV.

The problem is compounded by the relationship between politicians and journalists. Journalists are taught in their college classes that what a politician says is usually fit to be quoted, because it is news. For a politician, quotes and sound-bites are the stuff of re-election, and the hotter and more memorable, the better.

The result is a cycle of misinformation involving politicians, their staffs, and the mass media—very few of whom could give you a plausible explanation, off the top of their heads, of how an airplane stays up, let alone how Stealth works.

Enough editorializing. What follows is the most comprehensive and balanced account of the history, technology, and operational uses of the B-2 that I could put together. Read it and form your own opinions.

Chapter 1

Birth of a Bomber

"One-two-three! And where's your breakfast?"
Leopard stared, and Ethiopian stared, but all they could see were stripy
shadows and blotchy shadows in the forest, but never a sign of Zebra and
Giraffe.

—Rudyard Kipling, Just So Stories

It is no surprise that the Northrop B-2 is the most argued-about weapon of the nineties. The same dubious and often fatal distinction has haunted every bomber project that American aviators have tried to pursue, ever since the unquenchable Gen. Billy Mitchell declared the battleship obsolete in 1921.

The long-running bomber controversy is also the reason that US Air Force crews are still flying bombers designed forty-three years ago, the newest of which are more than three decades old. The strongest testimonial for the Boeing B-52, which the B-2 is intended to replace, is that it has taken so long to produce a replacement that seems to be worth the money.

The B-52 was the first intercontinental bomber of the nuclear age. Strategic Air Command (SAC) itself was formed in 1948, at which time its best in-service bomber was the World War II veteran B-29. In its formative years, SAC was closely identified with Gen. Curtis LeMay, who became its commander in October 1948. Rather than the cigar-chomping, bomb-happy monster of legend, LeMay was an innovative commander whose most usual criticism

was, "You can do better than that." (Its effect was often devastating.) He was also relentless in his war on slackness in any form, and had a keen sense of when to fire a subordinate to bring others into line.

Almost every unit in LeMay's experience had failed in its first mission, but for SAC there would be only one mission, and it had to be performed correctly. Under LeMay, SAC was transformed into an organization on a war footing. Its approach was summed up by a senior officer in 1988: "In Strategic Air Command, we work very hard to find the best way to do something; then, we all do it that way all the time." A standard joke is that if you open any desk in SAC, you will always find all the pencils in the same order.

Aviation technology surged ahead in the fifties, with LeMay's SAC firmly in the vanguard—confident that they could handle and operate any conceivable system, given enough training and the right leadership. First, SAC introduced the Boeing B-47, tricky to handle but capable of cruising as fast as most contemporary fighters. But only the slow, cannon-festooned B-36 could reach

Soviet targets from the United States, so in July 1948, USAF ordered prototypes of a faster replacement from Boeing.

Then, only three months later, the original turboprop-powered XB-52 design was thrown out in favor of a much faster aircraft using new jet engine technology. It flew in April 1952, and more than 700 were built in the fifties, along with a fleet of tankers to support them.

Even in 1952, SAC planners were working on the B-52's replacement: an intercontinental bomber designed to survive against a defensive system that would include supersonic, radar-equipped, missile-armed fighters; surface-to-air missiles (SAMs); long-range, early-warning radars; and the computer equipment needed to tie them together. The United States was developing such a system and there was no reason to assume that the Soviet Union would be far behind.

Some people already argued that the day of the manned bomber was passing. In 1946, the US Army Air Force (USAAF) had issued a contract to Northrop to develop the SM-62 Snark intercontinental cruise missile, which was to be followed by the Mach 3 North American SM-64 Navaho. Both of these programs, however, were overshadowed, overhauled, and eventually superseded by the intercontinental ballistic missile (ICBM). Missiles were faster than aircraft and their toughened re-entry vehicles were hard to destroy.

SAC continued to develop its bombers, making them more effective and more survivable. A vastly improved version of the B-52, the B-52G, could carry missiles to destroy defensive bases in its path and small decoys to confuse the defenders.

The ultimate replacement for the B-52 was supposed to be a supersonic, high-altitude bomber. The medium-range B-58 had been launched in early 1953 to replace the B-47; prototypes were ordered in the following year, and the first XB-58 flew in November 1956. A radical and complex aircraft, stuffed with extremely advanced electronic warfare and navigation equipment, the B-58 was designed to attack highly defended targets with a single multi-megaton thermonuclear weapon, making its bomb run at 55,000 feet and Mach 2 to evade the defenses.

Even the B-58 looked modest compared with what SAC wanted in a replacement for the B-52. The basic operational requirement, issued in October 1954, called for a 7,000-mile range, a 50,000-pound payload, and as high a speed over the target as possible; it was understood that SAC wanted Mach 2 or more.

Boeing and North American responded with designs featuring vast auxiliary fuel tanks attached to jettisonable outboard wing sections. Both proposals were rejected in March 1957, after new aerodynamic studies indicated that an aircraft could be designed to cruise at Mach 3 throughout its flight, meet the SAC payload-range requirement, and still be lighter than the subsonic-cruise designs. Both Boeing and North American re-submitted their proposals, and the latter's design was announced as the winner in December 1957.

The XB-70, named Valkyrie, was the most expensive and visible aircraft program of its day—as the B-52 had been before it. It was the heaviest aircraft in the world and, with the exception of the Central Intelligence Agency's secret Lockheed A-12, also the fastest.

But by the end of the fifties, the Pentagon was spending billions on land-based ICBMs and the Navy's submarine-launched Polaris missile. Compared with the missiles, even supersonic bombers seemed relatively easy to destroy, either on the ground or in the air. B-58 production stopped after 116 aircraft had been built. Production of the B-70 was canceled in 1959, reinstated in 1960, and finally canceled in 1961; two prototypes were built for research. The "whiz kids," the systems analysts who had been brought to the Pentagon by President Kennedy's defense secretary, Robert McNamara, expected that the B-52s would be scrapped by the end of the decade.

But the bomber proved harder to kill than anyone had expected. Any system that relies on ground-based radars has an Achilles heel: the radar cannot see beyond the horizon, and its range against low-flying targets is limited. At low level, the bomber could penetrate without warning and was much more difficult to track.

The implications for future bomber development were enormous. At low altitudes the air is so dense, relative to the air at normal cruising heights, that an aircraft cannot cruise efficiently above 650 mph, or Mach 0.9. The B-58, designed for Mach 2 cruise, was overdesigned and inefficient at such speeds, and the B-70 would be even worse off. At low altitude, the B-52 would easily outperform either supersonic aircraft, so the B-52s were strengthened and modified, while the B-58s went to the boneyard.

The switch to low-level operations meant that a new B-52 replacement would be completely different from the B-58 and B-70. Planning for such an aircraft started in 1962, as soon as it became clear that the B-70 would not be revived.

The next bomber, the USAF decided, would need to have better performance at low altitude. SAC still wanted the new bomber to be supersonic at high altitude, however, if only to force the

The B-2 will join the world's longest-serving combat aircraft, the Boeing B-52. This H-model is carrying AGM-129A Advanced Cruise Missiles under its port wing. Jim Burnett

Soviet defenses to keep their expensive, long-range missiles and high-altitude fighters in service.

By 1965, SAC's desired new strategic bomber looked like an extrapolated General Dynamics F-111, with a swing-wing and augmented turbofan engines. It would be three to four times bigger, however, to give it the necessary range and payload. Boeing, General Dynamics, and North American Rockwell were issued contracts to produce preliminary designs. Because "bomber" was still an explosive word on Capitol Hill and in the Office of the Secretary of Defense, the study was labeled as the Advanced Manned Strategic Aircraft (AMSA).

AMSA was to remain a study and nothing more as long as Robert McNamara had anything to do with it, and in the last three years of the Johnson administration the acronym was sometimes said to stand for "America's Most Studied Aircraft." The only bomber program launched in the sixties was a stopgap: the FB-111A, a slightly modified version of the tactical F-111E.

Flight testing of the FB-111A was well under way in November 1968, when Richard Nixon was elected president. His new secretary of defense, Melvin Laird, wasted no time in reversing McNamara's course. In March 1969, Laird announced that FB-111A production was to be stopped after seventy-four aircraft—four squadrons and spares— had been completed, and that more money would be provided for AMSA in 1969 and 1970.

Strategic planners had also come to realize that nuclear forces that relied almost entirely on missiles were dangerously unstable. It was almost impossible to construct such forces so that they could not be destroyed or crippled by a surprise attack. In such an event, the only way to preserve a missile force was

to fire as many missiles as possible as quickly as possible, pushing the force toward a hair-trigger "launch-on-warning" posture.

The answer was a concept called the Triad, combining bombers, sea-launched ballistic missiles (SLBMs), and ICBMs in a way that made a successful surprise attack impossible without resorting to launch on warning. Triad saw deterrence standing on three legs: ICBMs, SLBMs, and the bomber force— any one of which was capable of delivering a second strike that would threaten military targets and command centers.

Triad was a virtually ironclad guarantee against an effective first strike. Even at the lowest alert state, SAC could keep 30 percent of its bombers on alert, armed, fully fueled, and parked under heavy guard on alert pads adjacent to the end of their 15,000-foot runways. A thirty-bomber wing could get its ten alert bombers off the ground in well under ten minutes. In times of tension, training would stop and more bombers could be added to the alert force.

Any ICBMs the Soviet Union launched in a surprise attack against missile silos would be detected as soon as they left their silos, and the alert force would be airborne before they arrived. The Soviet planners could, alternatively, attack SAC bomber bases with low-trajectory SLBMs launched as closely as possible to the Atlantic coast, which would arrive much more quickly and allow fewer bombers to leave the ground. However, they could not do both. The SLBMs would hit long before the ICBMs arrived, and the United States could launch its full ICBM force. In either case, the United States could direct accurate ICBM or bomber strikes against military targets and US SLBMs would be kept in reserve. It was, simply, impossible to achieve an optimum first strike on both the bomber and ICBM legs of the Triad.

In November 1969, the USAF issued a request for proposals (RFP) for a new bomber. Six months later, the USAF selected Rockwell International, formerly North American, to develop the new bomber, designated the B-1A.

The USAF planned to build 240 B-1s, the first of them entering service late in the decade. The aircraft itself was so complex that it would take more than four years before the first prototype flew, and it was unlikely that the aircraft would see service long before 1980.

While carpenters and welders in Rockwell's El Segundo, California, fac-tory started to assemble an imposing full-size mock-up of the new bomber, some fundamental changes in aerospace technology were threatening to make the project obsolete.

Some of these changes were already reflected in a number of development programs, none of them very large and many of them highly secret. In small teams and small companies, aircraft designers, electrical engineers, computer specialists, operations analysts, and materials specialists were developing a radical approach to military aircraft design. It was so new that in 1970 it barely had a name, but it soon became known as Stealth.

In the fifties, SAC planned to replace sub-sonic bombers with aircraft capable of Mach 2 or more, like the B-58 Hustler. General Dynamics

Technically, Stealth was radical. Operationally, it represented only the latest stage in the struggle between the penetrating strike aircraft or bomber and the air defense system. Stealth was aimed at blurring the vision of the defender's most important sensor: radar.

Radar is basic to an air war. Before radar, air power theorists such as Italy's Gen. Guilio Douhet could argue that there was no practical defense against a massed bomber raid; the bombers would be overhead and attacking as soon as they could be detected and long gone before fighters could climb to meet them. But radar's first use was to provide early warning of a bombing raid, together with information about the raid's strength, speed, and track. In 1940— only a few years after aircraft detection was first demonstrated—the British used radar operationally in the Battle of Britain, and many historians believe that it was decisive.

Aircraft designers and air forces have taken drastic steps to negate radar. Most military aircraft carry some kind of radar warning system, which warns the crew that they have been detected. Virtually all combat aircraft carry jammers and chaff dispensers to protect themselves from radar-guided missiles. More powerful jammers are installed on special-purpose aircraft which either accompany the attacking force or stand off behind the battle area. A complete class of missiles has been developed to home on to radar emissions, either destroying the radar or forcing its operators to stop transmitting.

Compared with this array of weapons and technology, the idea of making the aircraft less detectable by radar in the first place seems so logical that it is not immediately obvious why Stealth is only now being put into practice.

It is not because the idea did not occur to anyone. The idea of radar camouflage is almost as old as radar itself. The first serious attempt to produce a warplane that would be significantly less visible to radar was made in 1943, and the idea of reducing the radar reflectivity of an aircraft was the subject of a great deal of research between the end of the 1939-45 war and the early seventies.

Sir Robert Watson-Watt, the pioneer of British radar, noted as early as 1935 that it would be logical for future heavy bombers to be designed so as to reduce their radar reflectivity. He was generally ignored. Most aircraft designers did not know how to measure the reflectivity of their aircraft and did not feel that it was important to do so.

Radar engineers, however, observed that their radars could detect targets at greater or lesser ranges, depending on the type of aircraft and the angle at which the radar beam struck it. This was a problem, because it frustrated efforts to measure and compare the performance of different radars. During the 1939-45 war, experiments were conducted to measure and plot the radar reflected from different targets. From this, the researchers derived measurements for radar cross-section (RCS).

The first aircraft designers to realize that differences in reflectivity could be tactically useful, and to attempt to reduce reflectivity in an aircraft design, were the brothers Walter and Reimar Horten in Germany. The Hortens were apostles of the flying wing, which they considered to be the ultimate in aerodynamic efficiency.

In 1943, the Horten brothers designed a twin-jet flying wing bomber and reconnaissance aircraft. Because of the shortage of materials, tools, and workers, a new aluminum aircraft from an unknown team had little chance of being approved for development in Germany. The Hortens proposed to build the new aircraft out of wood, with a central steel-tube subframe; the skins were to be made of two layers of thin plywood, sandwiched around a core made of glue, sawdust, and charcoal. The sole purpose of the charcoal was to absorb radar waves.

As it was eventually tested in 1944, the Horten HoIX had a conventional, non-absorbent plywood skin, but its design embodied a vital truth that was to elude designers until the late fifties.

During and after the war, researchers in America, Great Britain, and Germany continued to work on radar-absorbent material (RAM), trying to find a formula that would negate radar at minimal cost. Some types of RAM were used

operationally by the German Navy to shield the snorkel tubes of submarines from Allied airborne radars. In America, by 1945, a team at the Massachusetts Institute of Technology Radiation Laboratory had developed an "anti-radar paint" called MX-410. Actually a rubber material containing disc-like aluminum flakes, MX-410 proved to be an effective absorber, even in small layers.

Other rubber-based absorbers were developed by divisions of tire companies such as Goodyear and BF Goodrich. Most were used in static applications, not to prevent detection but to squelch unwanted reflections from structures close to a radar. Some, however, were produced in forms that were suitable for airborne use, and, in the fifties, a few aircraft, including a Lockheed U-2 and British Canberras, were treated with

Close behind the Hustler was the massive North American B-70 Valkyrie, with a Mach 3 *cruising speed and intercontinental range.* Rockwell

RAM and tested against air-defense radars.

The results were disappointing. The RCS reductions, achievable by applying RAM to a conventional aircraft, were insignificant or inconsistent. Given the trial-and-error nature of the tests, this was not surprising. Techniques for modeling and analyzing the radar returns produced by complex, real-world objects were inadequate, and designers did not realize that physically small parts of an aircraft could be disproportionately large radar reflectors.

In the late fifties, some designers rediscovered the truth onto which the Horten brothers had stumbled: that both shape and RAM are essential if a tactically useful RCS reduction is to be achieved. Aircraft manufacturers developed disciplined approaches to RCS control and devised ways of predicting the RCS of a new design before it was built.

Companies built RCS test ranges, where special radars illuminated large-scale models mounted on pylons, so that RCS predictions could be checked before an aircraft was built. By the early sixties, there were several such ranges in the United States, including a very large facility in New Mexico built by General Dynamics for the Air Force. Some companies established internal departments to develop specialized forms of RAM, and developed relationships with a growing group of companies specializing in absorber technology.

One of the leaders in this new discipline was Lockheed's Advanced Development Projects division, better known as the Skunk Works, under the leadership of its redoubtable founder, Clarence L. "Kelly" Johnson. Having carried out early installations of RAM on a U-2 (with little success), Johnson's team designed its successor, the Mach 3 A-12, with a low-RCS configuration and built-in RAM panels. It was the first successful attempt to reduce the RCS of a large aircraft; the A-12, almost as big as a B-58, was a much smaller radar target than any contemporary fighter.

The B-1 designers at Rockwell were aware of much of this early work. Rockwell itself had worked on RCS reduction in the early sixties, designing a low-RCS version of the Hound Dog missile, and the B-1 design reflected this experience. However, the Skunk Works team was on the edge of a leap forward: technology that would permit an aircraft to rely primarily on Stealth for its survival.

The problem with achieving very low RCS was that the interaction of the radar wave with the surface of the aircraft was very complex and beyond the scope of human computation. Even with the more powerful mainframe computers available in the early seventies, the compound-curved shapes of an airplane's skin presented near-insoluble scattering problems.

Nevertheless, by 1975 enough progress had been made for the USAF to convene a classified symposium on "radar camouflage" at Wright-Patterson Air Force Base. It was a pivotal event, pointing towards solutions for many of the tough problems. Shortly afterwards, the Defense Advanced Research Projects Agency (DARPA) asked General Dynamics and Northrop to propose designs for an ultra-low-RCS demonstrator aircraft. It was named Project Harvey, after the invisible, six-foot-tall rabbit that haunted James Stewart in the movie of that name. Project Harvey was unclassified.

General Dynamics and Northrop, however, were defeated by an unsolicited bid from Lockheed. The Skunk Works engineers' breakthrough was that they threw out the conventions of aircraft design by eliminating curved surfaces

Thirty years after accepting the first B-52, SAC took delivery of a new long-range bomber, the Rockwell B-1B, with swing-wings *to permit high-speed flight at low level.* Rockwell

from the airplane's shape. The only reason for doing this was to simplify the RCS problem, to the point where a state-of-the-art Control Data computer, running a newly developed program called Echo, could model the RCS of the airframe over a wide range of frequencies and at any angle. The result was an extraordinary aircraft with a faceted outer surface, like a cut diamond.

Before much work had been done, Project Harvey was transferred to the USAF and renamed XST (experimental, stealth, tactical). Lockheed and Northrop were asked to design XST prototypes and build full-scale models for testing on the New Mexico range. In mid-1976, Lockheed's design was selected and work began on two prototypes, now codenamed Have Blue, under a $45 million contract.

The results of the model tests electrified those who knew about them. If Stealth worked as well as it appeared to, it could render every defensive system in the world obsolete—including those of the United States. The USAF immediately threw the heaviest possible cloak of secrecy over everything to do with Stealth, while forming a small, high-level study group to consider what to do with this new technology.

The first of the Have Blue aircraft flew in January or February of 1978, and although both were destroyed in accidents, they proved that an ultra-low-observables aircraft could fly. The new technology captured the attention of President Jimmy Carter's new administration, winning allies in Defense Secretary Harold Brown and William Perry, defense undersecretary of research and engineering.

Meanwhile, the B-1's prospects had plunged. The first B-1 had rolled out at Palmdale in October 1974, but the program was already late and over budget and critics were advocating a cheaper alternative: the small, relatively inexpensive, long-range cruise missile. Proponents argued that the cruise missile could overwhelm Soviet defenses by weight of numbers, and that it could be launched from B-52s or inexpensive transport aircraft.

The B-1 continued to survive votes in Congress, by a narrow margin, and in December 1976, the Department of Defense approved production of 240 B-1s. The first of these would be delivered in 1979 and become operational in mid-1982. The timing made it clear, however, that this was merely a gesture by the lame-duck Ford administration, forcing President Carter to confront the issue.

In June 1977, Carter canceled the B-1 production program. Most of the B-1 money would be shifted into full-scale development of the cruise missile and a new navigation system for the B-52G/H bombers that would carry it.

Once again, however, the reports of the bomber's death proved exaggerated. One of the four B-1 prototypes was completed and used for a series of "bomber penetrativity evaluation" tests, conducted at Nellis Air Force Base in 1979. They produced some remarkable results. At 600 mph, 250 feet above the ground, following a winding track

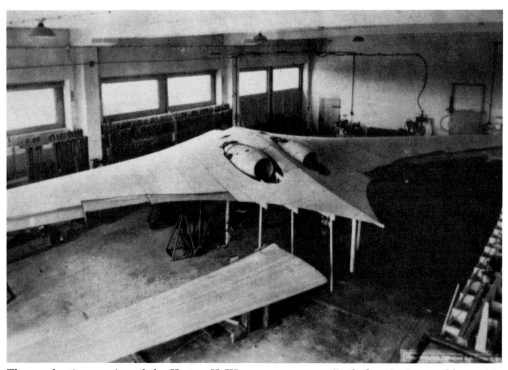

The production version of the Horten HoIX would have been skinned with a radar-absorbing plywood sandwich material, one of many ways (including its internal layout) in which it foreshadowed the B-2. Motor-Buch Verlag

around and over the Nevada mountains, and making extensive use of jamming. the B-1 proved very hard to track. The control centers frequently had no idea where the intruder was until it popped up over the hills on its final attack run. The tests were a big step forward for the manned bomber's advocates in the USAF, the higher levels of the Pentagon, and Congress.

Meanwhile, engineers and strategic analysts studied a whole range of strategic weapon systems, ranging from cruise-missile-carrying transports to versions of the B-1 and radically altered FB-111As.

The most radical new bomber proposals resulted from a program called Saber Penetrator. This study assumed that the B-52 or another aircraft would be used to carry cruise missiles, perform Vietnam-type heavy bombing missions, or launch anti-shipping missiles, and called for an all-new bomber designed specifically to penetrate Soviet airspace; it was to use the most advanced technology in prospect, and need not be in service before the nineties. Not surprisingly, the resulting proposals combined advanced aerodynamics, new materials, and—above all—Stealth. Saber Penetrator resulted in a series of bomber designs, some of them flying wings.

Already, during 1977, the USAF's Stealth group had identified the priority uses for Stealth technology: first, a Stealth strike fighter that could be fielded as quickly as possible; second, Stealth strategic weapons for use against the Soviet Union. These would be a cruise missile and a bomber. By late 1978, with early Have Blue results in hand, the low-observables group had awarded study contracts for Stealth strategic bombers to both Lockheed and Northrop.

Lockheed had built the Have Blue prototypes and, in late 1978, had signed a contract to develop the operational F-117A—but what of Northrop? Anyone who had suggested in 1978 that Northrop could make a serious run for prime-contractor status on the next strategic bomber would have been quietly removed from the scene and tested for controlled substances. The only manned aircraft that Northrop had built in numbers for years was the F-5, a lightweight fighter produced almost entirely for export to allies unable to afford the bigger and more potent machines used by the USAF. Northrop had not built a combat aircraft for front-line USAF service since 1958.

But there was more to Northrop than met the eye. Run by a core group of highly experienced, long-serving engineer/managers, the company had a reputation for advanced thinking. Its chairman and chief executive officer, Thomas V. Jones (who had been president or chairman since 1959), had helped to originate the concept of "life cycle cost" (LCC) at Northrop in the fifties; by estimating the complete cost of flying and maintaining a fleet of aircraft throughout its active life, LCC analysis showed whether a given design change would cost more or less in the long run.

One of Northrop's leading designers, Lee Begin, had been designing highly agile fighters in the mid-sixties, before the USAF realized how badly it needed them. (Begin's design eventually entered service as the F-18 Hornet.) The company was less reluctant than most aerospace companies to build and equip new plants or to invest its own money in promising ideas; the most conspicuous example was its F-20, the only US fighter since the fifties to be built with private money. (The last private-venture fighter before then had been the first Northrop F-5.) Northrop had also grown, through acquisitions and internal development, into an unusually broad-based military aerospace company, with divisions producing advanced navigation systems, electronic countermeasures equipment, and unmanned aircraft.

And, in the mid-sixties, Northrop began to concentrate on Stealth, researching shapes and materials and commissioning the test facilities which the new discipline required. "As a company, we set a course a long time ago, and we stuck to it," chairman Jones remarked at the company's 1988 annual meeting. "We agreed that Northrop would concentrate on fundamental technologies which, if we were successful, would someday—years later, perhaps—be essential for our customers' and our country's success." Important advances were achieved, according to the company's 1988 annual report. "The essential breakthrough by Northrop engineers and scientists involved the ability to design low observability into combat aircraft without compromising aircraft capability," Northrop stated. In the mid-seventies, Northrop began hiring more engineers with experience in low observables.

The Northrop Stealth group was led by John Cashen, Irving Waaland, and John Patierno. Most significantly, Cashen was an electrical engineer. ("E. E.'s" had been a low form of life in the design office for most of the history of aviation, concerned mainly with wiring and circuitbreakers.) The scattering theory that underlies Stealth is fundamentally an electrical problem, and Cashen was the first of many electrical specialists to oust the aerodynamicist as the king of the design group.

Northrop had lost the Have Blue contest to Lockheed, but now it was Northrop's turn to achieve a breakthrough. Using new software run on the new, ultra-fast supercomputers developed by Cray Research, the company's engineers refined shaping techniques to make Stealth possible without faceting the surfaces. Drag could be reduced substantially and the payload and range increased, particularly important advantages for a strategic bomber.

Northrop was awarded a contract to build and test a prototype aircraft to demonstrate its "seamless" Stealth design approach. Powered by four jet engines buried in the wings, it was tested in 1981 at the USAF's secret Groom Lake flight-test base in Nevada; its bluff contours won it the nickname Shamu.

In June 1979, veteran designer Hal Markarian produced for Northrop's Stealth group a sketch of a flying wing bomber with a straight-edged planform and overwing inlets feeding the buried engines: six of them at this point, because the bomber had very slim side and front profiles. As the design developed, however, it grew deeper and more capacious, until it could hold as much weaponry as a B-52 and deliver it over an equal or greater distance.

Meanwhile, the USAF was assessing the threat and beginning to question whether the B-1 could be an effective penetrator in the late nineties and beyond. In the Soviet Union, Mikoyan was developing a new Ye-155MP area-defense interceptor with a heavy armament and powerful radar to accompany the new missiles with hard-to-jam monopulse phased-array radars. These new weapons would make jamming more difficult and diminish the protection of terrain cover that the B-1 was designed to exploit.

The effect of Stealth on the USAF's thinking was dramatic. By mid-1979, only two years after the B-1 had been canceled, SAC Commander Gen. Richard H. Ellis no longer regarded its resurrection as a high priority. SAC's preferred "roadmap" for its bomber force was to continue the B-52-plus-cruise-missile program and, as quickly as possible, to develop the enlarged F-111 into 155 modified FB-111H aircraft, while launching a long, careful program to develop a Stealth bomber for the nineties.

However, the SAC plan was not backed by the higher echelons of the USAF command, where the B-1 still enjoyed considerable support. Both SAC and the USAF headquarters believed that the Stealth bomber was the best long-term choice for the penetrator role, but that the B-52H, SAC's best in-service penetrating bomber, would be outclassed by Soviet defenses before the new aircraft could be ready. However, while SAC considered that 155 FB-111Hs were equal to 100 B-1s, the USAF command decided to ask for both a resurrected B-1, incorporating some Stealth technology, and a Stealth bomber.

The Stealth bomber concept gained momentum in 1979. The Iranian revolution, the taking as hostages the US

The Horten brothers even designed an intercontinental flying wing bomber, the HoXVIII.
Motor-Buch Verlag

embassy staff in Tehran, and the Soviet Union's invasion of Afghanistan reinforced the impression that the world was a dangerous place. With the impending election, Carter sought to shake off the "soft on defense" label pinned on him by his opponents, and proposed an increased defense budget that—buried under secret code names and unexplained line items—contained hundreds of millions of dollars for Stealth aircraft.

Some of this money was to be used to start the new bomber. In September 1980, the USAF issued an RFP to Northrop and Lockheed, covering development of the Advanced Strategic Penetrator Aircraft (ASPA) and production of 132 aircraft.

The RFP called for ASPA to perform the full spectrum of bomber missions, including nuclear strike, conventional bombing, anti-shipping and armed maritime patrol, and sea mining. It had to be capable of surviving unsupported against any projected defense system, and its avionics and sensors had to be capable of detecting mobile targets.

Proposals were submitted in December. Northrop's design, code named Senior Ice, resembled Markarian's flying wing, while Lockheed's Senior Peg was reminiscent of the F-117A, with some faceting still evident.

By this time, Northrop was teamed with Boeing and LTV, and Lockheed had joined with Rockwell. Teaming served many purposes. A project the size of the ATB was too large for a single company to handle. Even if it was possible for a company to expand its workforce and facilities to do much of the work in-house, it would probably not be efficient; and even if a company could do the job efficiently, the termination of the project could destroy it.

Northrop's ASPA team members brought their own strengths to the party. Boeing Military Airplane Company knew large aircraft and large programs. LTV was unusual in that it had deliberately withdrawn from developing and building new aircraft in favor of improving its abilities as a subcontractor to other companies. It was already investing heavily in new technologies, such as computer-aided manufacturing of composite materials and industrial robotics.

Both of Northrop's team members were also major subcontractors on the B-1, and were hedging their bets in case Rockwell's bid to sell B-1s failed. The public bomber debate continued during 1981. Rockwell promised a reduced, fixed price for the B-1, and the proponents of the Stealth bomber promised better performance and early delivery dates. Secretary of Defense Caspar Weinberger was unconvinced of the need to develop two new bombers.

Nevertheless, this was the solution chosen by the Reagan administration and announced on October 20, 1981. Production of 100 B-1Bs would start immediately; it would be a fast-paced effort, with the first new bomber to be delivered in 1984 and the last in 1988. The B-1B would start to replace the B-52H in the penetrator mission by 1986, and the B-52s would, in turn, be converted to launch cruise missiles.

Northrop's team was awarded the $7,300 million contract to start development of the Stealth bomber, now known as the Advanced Technology Bomber (ATB). Its code name was Senior CJ, and it would later acquire the official designation B-2. (The code name honored Connie Jo Kelly, the secretary of the low-observables group.) Entering service in the nineties, the B-2 would replace the B-1B as a penetrator, and the B-1Bs

Northrop's spectacular YB-49 was the ultimate flying wing of the forties. Hampered by control problems, an inability to carry nuclear weapons, and its roots in the slower, *piston-engined XB-35 design, the YB-49 was passed over in favor of the faster B-47 and larger B-36.* Northrop

would be reassigned as cruise missile launchers.

It was the most expensive way of acquiring 240 new bombers that had been proposed. It is far cheaper to build 240 aircraft of one type than to split the same total for two different aircraft, each requiring a massive non-recurring investment. There were a number of reasons for the two-bomber program, including some outright political considerations.

As a presidential candidate from California, Ronald Reagan had savagely criticized Carter's cancellation of the B-1A and had promised to resurrect it, unaware of the greater promise of the still-secret B-2. Also, 1984 would bring another election, and, possibly, another Democratic administration. The Democrats had won the White House from the Republicans twice in recent years (1960 and 1976), and, in both cases, a new USAF bomber had been dead within a year. The B-2, in the middle of a long

development process, would be ripe for the same treatment, but the B-1B would be so far along in production that it would be much harder to kill.

Publicly, the Air Force and the Pentagon talked about the "window of vulnerability," arguing that improvements in Soviet air defenses would render the B-52H incapable of penetrating its targets by the mid-to-late-eighties, before the Stealth bomber could be ready; an "interim penetrator" was therefore required urgently. By the early-to-mid-nineties, however, improved defenses would be able to stop the interim aircraft. The B-1B was the logical solution, since, unlike the improved FB-111, it could be adapted to other heavy bomber missions once its career as a penetrator was over.

Defense Secretary Weinberger, less convinced of the merits of Stealth than some of Carter's advisors, saw the B-1B as a back-up to the B-2 in case the new bomber hit trouble or even failed completely. The B-2 program was set up to reduce risks, and the in-service date was set for the early nineties; Stealth advocates had claimed the new bomber could be in service by 1987.

The bomber administration plan was laid out to avoid drastic peaks in funding and to keep the technical risks under control. Spending on the B-1 would "ramp up" very quickly from 1982 until 1985; after then, it would decline as the production line shut down. While B-1B spending was at its highest, Northrop and its partners would complete the design of the B-2. The big investments in full-scale development— designing every part of the aircraft— and preparations for production would come later.

The B-2 was to make its first flight in December 1987 and become operational in 1991 or 1992. With the B-1 in hand, however, the USAF was prepared to use the timetable as a tool, rather than letting the schedule drive the program. Instead of pouring money onto a problem or forging ahead with the program, hoping that a solution would be found and that it would not require major rework, the USAF was prepared to let the schedule slip if a better aircraft could be obtained at lower risk.

If, by early 1985, the B-2 had proved to be less capable or far more expensive than anticipated, the USAF would have the option of changing requirements or extending the schedule, while buying more B-1s if the military situation at the time made it necessary.

The existence of the B-1 also allowed the USAF to push for the best B-2 possible, without worrying as much about the schedule as it would have to do if there was no modern bomber in the force. In particular, the USAF intended to produce one, definitive version of the B-2 that would require little develop-

ment apart from improved computer software after it entered service.

There were certainly areas of high risk in the B-2's radical design. These included the unconventional engine inlets and exhausts, the design's Stealth characteristics, its stability and controllability, and the technology required to build the new bomber in such a way that it would retain its Stealth qualities for decades.

Where the risks could be identified, Northrop and the USAF defined "risk closure" programs. These defined ways of exploring the risk areas—through rig, simulation, and wind-tunnel tests, for example—and set standards by which the program leaders would know that the risks had been reduced to an acceptable level. Only then would they make final, critical design decisions that would cost billions to reverse.

Another reason that the USAF was able to accept delays on the B-2 program was that such a decision would not produce banner headlines, as would be the case for most other projects. This was because the entire program was secret. From the start of the project until early 1988, unclassified information on the B-2 program amounted to a few dozen words. Northrop, Boeing, LTV, and General Electric could be identified as the main contractors, 132 aircraft were to be built, and the bomber was described as incorporating low-observable technology: that was all that the USAF was prepared to say.

At no time in recent history has the Pentagon told the US public about all of its projects. The existence of entire programs is classified and whole classes of equipment are classified, so that any new system in that category is automatically secret. Devices and systems for spying on potential adversaries, for example, are secret. As a result, any new

Northrop proposed this delta-wing design with a top inlet for the USAF's XST program, *but the USAF chose Lockheed's more radical design.* Northrop

technology applicable to strategic reconnaissance is secret by definition.

Such projects are unofficially called "black programs," but are more correctly called Special Access Required (SAR) programs, after the security regulations covering them. An SAR program is open only to those with specific clearance, identified by the program's code name; this clearance is based on a "need to know," regardless of the individual's seniority. Information in an SAR program is "compartmentalized": people working in one area know no more than they need to know about the project as a whole, and those at higher levels are not routinely cleared to know all of the details of the work they supervise.

The B-2 was not as "black" as some projects: its existence was acknowledged and some information was released from the outset. What made the B-2 project different was its sheer size and the number of companies involved in it. Northrop's first security measure was to remove the project from the rest of the organization, forming a separate division—Advanced Products—and acquiring a closed-down Ford plant at Pico Rivera to house it. The plant was quickly surrounded by fences topped with coiled wire, bristling with razorlike blades.

Security measures at Pico Rivera and other plants have been described as paranoid, but, as the proverb has it, "Being paranoid doesn't mean that they're not out to get you." Before the B-2 contract was awarded, a Polish intelligence officer recruited an engineer at Hughes Radar Systems Group, William Bell, and obtained details of the company's work on "quiet" radar systems, such as the B-2's. (Bell was sentenced to eight years in prison in 1981.) There was

Lockheed's success in developing the F-117A from the Have Blue demonstrator converted many skeptics to belief in Stealth, and paved the way for a Stealth bomber program. Lockheed

no way to guarantee that other employees would not be approached and turned by foreign agents. Instead, security measures within the razor-wire perimeter were designed to minimize the damage that any one spy could cause.

Compartmentalization is enforced by means ranging from twenty-first century gadgetry to Biblical simplicity. The latter is typified by the procedures used when a person visits an area where he or she is not cleared into the details of the work (a computer specialist visits an engineering office, for example). The visitor is escorted, a light flashes above the visitor's location, and the escort rings a bell, announcing "Uncleared person in area!"

Secure facilities include conference rooms, with double sound-proof doors and motion detectors (so that no agent can plant a bug while the conference room is unoccupied). Computers are a necessity but a serious security risk because they leak electromagnetic signals that can be decoded. (The Pentagon has a standard for computer security, called Tempest, but this had not been defined when the B-2 program started.) Any computers handling sensitive information are housed in metal-lined rooms, also equipped with double doors. Employees and visitors are forbidden to carry personal microcassette recorders and even, in some cases, pocket calculators, because any electronic device could disguise some kind of bug.

Individual rooms are fitted with programmable combination locks and sealed to Tempest standards against electronic leaks. Even the heating and air-conditioning ducts are fitted with steel blocker bars and motion sensors to prevent inter-program intrusion.

The three associate contractors on the B-2 who were identified by the USAF were not permitted to divulge their roles in the program. Other companies were not even named, but the subcontractor list included hundreds of large and small concerns across the United States.

The Southern California aerospace industry is dominated by such giants as Northrop and Lockheed, but it also relies on dozens of small job shops producing electronic or structural components to order, in lots that might be uneconomical for a large company. In some cases, Northrop set up cover companies so that these small subcontractors, which do not have the facilities to support high-security work, would not be aware that their components were destined for Pico Rivera.

There were many good reasons for concealing the technical details of the B-2 program. The bomber included so many radical features that it presented the Soviet Union with a challenge of unknown magnitude, while its Stealth design meant that its external shape could provide clues to its detectability. This was important: outside the security cordon, few people could believe that the Northrop and Lockheed designers had achieved the vast reductions in RCS that had, in fact, already been demonstrated.

What was more controversial was the decision to conceal the costs of the B-2 program from the public. The unclassified versions of annual Pentagon budget requests include sums in the billions of dollars for programs identified only by code names such as Senior Citizen or Have Trump. Further billions are hidden under such titles as "advanced concepts" or "selected activities." Both the code names and the cover phrases change from year to year, so there is no way to track these expenditures. By 1987, one investigation by the *Philadelphia Inquirer* put the black budget at $35 billion, or eleven per cent of the total Pentagon budget. The figure was three times as high as it had been in 1981.

While the detailed breakdown of these totals is secret from the public, the Pentagon maintains that democratic process has not been circumvented, because expenses are still overseen by Congress. The members of the House and Senate Armed Services Committees have special security clearances that give them access to the uncensored Pentagon budgets.

By late 1988, the only cost figure released by the USAF was a $36.6 billion "program cost" in 1981 dollars. The USAF argued that the flow of money into a program gives away its size and its timescale to an adversary. However, the size of the B-2 program—132 aircraft—has never been secret. While its schedule may have been uncertain, plus or minus two years, in the early stages of the program, it was fairly obvious by 1985—as a huge assembly plant arose at Palmdale, behind double razor-wire fences—that the earliest service-entry date would be 1992.

Also in 1988, the USAF began to lift the veil on Stealth. From the beginning,

This Boeing study for a Stealth bomber was released in 1980, just before a shroud of secrecy was thrown over the entire subject of Stealth. *This aircraft is smaller than the B-2, and was probably designed to deliver four gravity bombs or SRAMs. Boeing*

the service had recognized that there was no way to conceal 132 large bombers from the public eye. For this reason, only a few years of concealment could be bought by attempting to hide the prototypes.

This in itself would be expensive, demanding the construction of a new, separate final assembly plant at a secure site, such as Groom Lake in Nevada. Moreover, ferrying hundreds of assembly-line workers into Groom could compromise the security of the whole facility. Instead, the B-2 would be revealed when it was ready to fly.

On November 22, 1988, hangar doors opened at Palmdale and B-2 air vehicle 1 (AV-1) was pulled into the light of day, resembling nothing so much as a strange sea creature dragged from its lair.

A notable feature of this Rockwell design, of the same vintage as the Boeing study, is the radar installation in the wing leading edge. Rockwell

Chapter 2

Under the Skin

Any reasonable assumptions will always result in an advantage to the all-wing configuration, of such magnitude as to fully warrant whatever trials and tribulations may be involved in its development.

—John K. "Jack" Northrop, 1947

When the B-2 rolled out, it was the first time that the aircraft, or any one of its major components, had been seen by anyone who had not been sworn to secrecy, under penalty of incarceration. The dramatic effect was undeniable, because the B-2 looks like no other vehicle in the history of aviation.

The only airplanes that have ever looked remotely like the B-2 were flown in the forties, when designers in the United States, Great Britain, and Germany were pursuing the idea of an all-wing airplane or flying wing. As its name suggests, the all-wing airplane has neither fuselage nor tail, but carries all of its payload, fuel, and components inside the wing. Even those distant ancestors, though, did not share the single dominating, most bizarre feature of the B-2's shape.

Viewed from directly above or below, the B-2's boomerang-like shape comprises twelve ruler-straight lines. The leading edges, the long sides of the boomerang, run straight from the extreme nose to the extreme tips of the wing. The wingtips are not parallel with the airflow, like those on most normal airplanes, but are cut off at a near-right-angle to the leading edges. Apart from the tips, the outer wings have no taper; another deviation from normal aircraft. The inner trailing edges form a jagged shape, jutting backwards toward the centerline. A closer inspection shows that the edges form two groups of six exactly parallel lines.

Look at the B-2 from any point on the horizontal plane, however, and the shape changes. In front, rear, or side view, the bomber has virtually no straight lines and no hard edges. The top and bottom surfaces are both continuous, three-dimensional curved surfaces. Even the over-wing air inlets, which look jagged from a distance, can be seen at close range to be made up of many curved segments. There are even very few curves of constant radius; rather, the surfaces change radius continuously, as though they were produced from segments of a spiral. The shape has no abrupt distinctions between body and wing; a dorsal hump with the cockpit in front rises smoothly from the top surface, but the underside swells gradually from the outermost trailing edge kink to the centerline.

Combined with the things that the eye expects to see but are not there—engine pods, a fuselage, a vertical fin, and a stabilizer—the effect is that the B-2 looks like something organic rather than a machine: an immense manta ray, improbably resting on its wheels in the high desert of California.

Stealth Design

Nothing in aircraft design is accidental, and very little is influenced by convention and much less by style. The size and shape of an aircraft is the result of a compromise hammered out by the requirements of the job that the aircraft has to do.

There is a cartoon, not much younger than the airplane itself, that is probably found in every aircraft design office in the world. It shows an aircraft as each group in the team wants to design it. The aerodynamics group's design is slender, smooth, and flowing. The production group's contribution is usually represented by four planks, nailed together in the shape of an airplane. The maintenance group's design is a mass of access panels, with all the control cables and hydraulic pipes on the outside.

The point that the cartoon makes is that none of the designs is workable in itself. The different groups have to compromise, or "trade," accepting less-than-optimum in one area to meet minimum requirements in another. Speed, range, payload, and what engineers call "-ilities"—reliability, maintainability, supportability—are all part of the "trade studies" in the earliest stages of design. What makes the B-2 look so strange is the simple fact that a completely new and very important "-ility" was added to the trade studies back in 1978: observability.

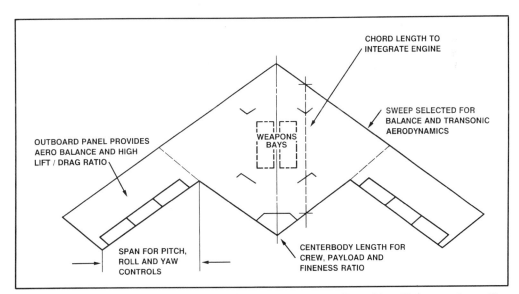

The original B-2 design was built around a number of key dimensions, to provide space for the crew, weapons bays, and engines in a neutrally stable, efficient package. Note that all the elevons are on the outer wing.
Northrop

That said, Stealth differs from other design qualities in a number of important ways. It works only when it is given high priority, so that the aircraft is not just twice as difficult to detect as a conventional type, but ten or a hundred times more so. When it is applied in such a way, Stealth tends to be the main driver behind the design, just as sustained Mach 3 performance was the main driver in the design of the SR-71. Unlike some technologies, such as new materials or electronics, Stealth directly affects the outside shape of the airplane. For these reasons, Stealth aircraft look drastically different from other aircraft.

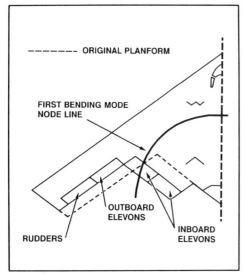

The B-2 was redesigned in 1983 to allow it to fly faster at low level. Because the elevons act to counter the effects of air turbulence, it was necessary to add inboard elevons at a stiffer part of the wing. At the same time, that part of the trailing edge was extended aft to give the new elevons enough leverage, creating the B-2's jagged trailing edge. Finally, the outer wings were made more slender, to offset the increased drag of the added wing area inboard. Northrop

According to Ben Rich, leader of the Lockheed team that created the F-117, "a Stealth aircraft has to be stealthy in six disciplines: radar, infrared, visual, acoustic, smoke, and contrail. If you don't do that, you flunk the course."

If this is the case, why do most studies of Stealth concentrate on radar? The answer is that the importance that you assign to each of the six disciplines depends on the threat that you are facing. A ground-hugging military helicopter is likely to be heard before a radar can pick it up and is more likely to be targeted by an infrared (IR) homing weapon than a radar-directed one, so acoustic and thermal signatures are important. A submarine is a perfect example of a system that is stealthy in the acoustic spectrum, almost exclusively.

Military airplanes, however, face their greatest threat from radar. Radar can pick an airplane up at a greater distance than any other sensor; large airborne or ground-based early-warning radars have an effective range of 200 to 300 miles, and the only reason that they are not built with greater range is that they run into line-of-sight limits against most targets. The range of the best IR system (the closest competitor) is in the high tens of miles under ideal conditions.

Unlike IR, radar gives a very precise estimate of the target's position, can track the changes in a target's position, and can determine its speed and course, both of which are essential to achieving an interception. Emerging radar technology, using high-speed processors to analyze the return radar signal in ways that would have taken hours of computer time a few years ago, can even find ways to identify the type of aircraft on the screen.

Applied to military aircraft, Stealth means reducing two things: the range at which radar can detect the aircraft, and the level of observables in the other five categories to the point where the detection range in those spectra is not significantly greater, whatever combination of available or forecast technologies may be used.

Radar Cross-Section

All radar systems, from an AWACS to a police speed radar, work in the same way. A radio-frequency signal is transmitted through a directional antenna that focuses it into a conical beam. When a reflective target (in radar jargon, anything observed by radar is a target) blocks part of the beam, that part of the beam is reflected in many different directions, or is "scattered." Mostly, the scattering is complex and rapidly varying, so that it is effectively random and

some energy will be reflected in the direction of the radar antenna.

Most radars transmit energy in pulses, thousands of them every second; in the gaps between the pulses, the radar becomes a receiver, and the gaps are long enough for the signal to make its way to the target and back at the speed of light. The interval between the transmission and reception of the pulse gives the range from the radar to the target. The radar antenna moves at a regular rate, so the time at which the target moves in and out of the beam can be tied to the position of the antenna, giving the target's bearing from the location of the radar.

Radar sees only the energy that is reflected towards it, and it can detect a target only when the antenna captures enough energy to rise above the elec-

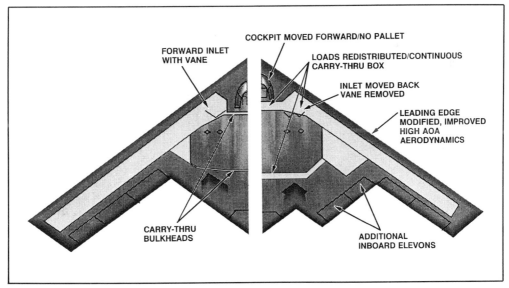

With the new wing design (right), Northrop also changed the internal structure so that much more of the load would be borne by two massive spars or "carry-through boxes" fore and aft of the weapons bay. The cockpit was moved forward and the inlets aft, to clear the internal structure. The change relieved the loads on the bomber's composite skin, which is, nonetheless, one inch thick in some parts of the centerbody section. Northrop

31

tronic noise that is present in the receiver. All the variables in the transmission-scattering-reception chain affect the maximum range at which this can happen; these variables include the strength of the signal, the width of the beam, the size of the antenna, and the radar cross-section (RCS) of the target.

Target RCS is the one variable that the target's designer alone can affect. The relationship of RCS to the detection range is not in direct proportion, because of the conical beam and radial scattering effects. Detection range is in proportion to the fourth root of RCS. If a radar has a range of 100 miles against a

target with an RCS of $10m^2$ its range will be 85 miles against a target of half the reflectivity ($5m^2$). A $1m^2$ RCS translates into a 55-mile detection range. A 90 per cent reduction in reflectivity equals a 45 per cent reduction in detection range— hardly a very inspiring feature.

What makes Stealth possible is that far larger reductions in target RCS are achievable, because conventional, unstealthy aircraft are almost ideal radar targets.

To the radar wave, conductive surfaces are like mirrors. A conventional aircraft has a complex external shape,

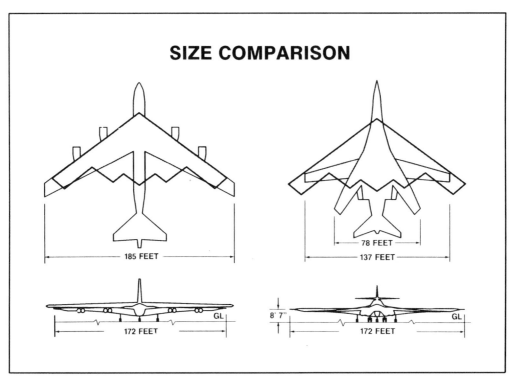

SIZE COMPARISON

185 FEET

172 FEET

78 FEET

137 FEET

8' 7"

172 FEET

The B-2 has almost the same wingspan and a slightly greater wing area than the B-52, but is some fifty tons lighter at its maximum takeoff weight. The B-2 weighs about the same as a B-1B, in clean condition, but has much more wing area and span. The result is that it is more efficient than either. USAF

full of curves, flat panels, and edges, and is a pseudo-random scatterer. As it moves relative to a radar illuminating it, an airplane throws off a constantly changing, scintillating pattern of concentrated reflections.

RCS is based on the size of a reflective sphere (the optical equivalent would be a spherical mirror) that would return the same amount of energy as the object in question. The RCS is the projected area of that sphere, or the area of a disk of the same diameter.

A small, efficient reflector—such as a flat plate, normal to the radar beam—reflects as much energy as a very large sphere. A square plate, 10cm by 10cm (3.937in), has an area of 0.01m². Its RCS, when it is normal to the radar beam, is 1m² or 100 times as large as the actual plate. Compound shapes can be worse. Reflective panels at 90deg to one another can turn a radar signal through two right-angles and fire it back to the receiver in full intensity.

Many modern aircraft are full of such reflectors, and the resulting RCS figures are almost staggering. Viewed from the side, a typical fighter, such as the F-15 Eagle, may have a projected area of 25m². Because of the aircraft's design, however, the side RCS may be sixteen times as large, at 400m², or the size of a very large house. Typical frontal-aspect RCS figures for modern aircraft run around 10m² for fighters, and 1,000m² for a bomber such as the B-52 or a transport aircraft such as the 747.

It follows that the Stealth designer's creed starts with the same words as the physician's Hippocratic oath: "First, do no harm." Some popular design features are incompatible with low RCS.

Engines in external pods or hung on pylons, such as those of the B-52, provide many excellent radar reflectors. Vertical stabilizers and slab-sided bodies are ruled out. External stores are equally unacceptable.

Although a flat plate has a huge RCS if it is normal to the radar beam, the reverse is also true. As the plate is tilted or canted away from the beam in one dimension, its RCS decreases sharply: reflectivity is reduced by a factor of 1,000 (30 dB) at a cant angle of 30deg. But if the same surface is rotated away from the beam on a diagonal axis—that is to say, it is both canted and swept back—the RCS reduction is much greater, so that a 30 dB reduction can be realized at an 8deg angle.

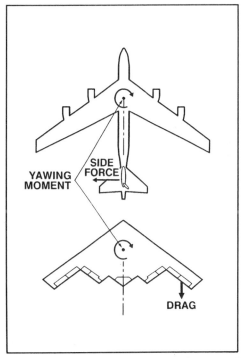

Many aircraft have no separate horizontal tail, including the commercially certificated Concorde. With no vertical tail, the B-2 is unique among modern aircraft. Instead, yaw is controlled by differential drag rudder/ brakes at the wingtips. Northrop

The Stealth designer can take advantage of the fact that the most threatening radar systems will illuminate his aircraft from a point, at most, ten miles below it or ten miles above it, but at a much greater distance than that. Most radar waves will impinge on the target from a narrow range of shallow angles. If as much as possible of the surface of the aircraft is highly oblique to those angles, preferably in both tilt and rotation, the RCS will be low, because most of the energy will be scattered. This can be accomplished by sloping the body sides or by blending the body into the wing.

Engines produce strong radar reflections and have to be concealed in some way, while permitting air to reach the engine efficiently. The basic idea of a stealth inlet is to cause any radiation entering the duct to bounce as many times as possible off the sides before it is reflected out again, using RAM to absorb energy with each bounce. With a little skill, the number of bounces can be increased significantly without sacrific-

This is not a mad sculptor's studio but a radar cross-section measurement range, large enough to handle large-scale models and full-scale parts such as antennas. The "target" is mounted on the pylon at left, while the jagged plate against the far wall is a reflector that focuses the radar beam on to the target. The transmitter is housed in the short tower in front of the reflector. Similar ranges were used in the development of the B-2. Lockheed

ing aerodynamic performance. However, this tends to demand a long, complex inlet system, which takes up a great deal of space. The ban on external stores puts more pressure on internal volume. A Stealth aircraft needs a shape with plenty of volume but not too much external surface area.

Flying Wings

By 1943 (only five years after the first air-defense radars had been built) the Horten brothers realized that the flying wing met all these basic Stealth requirements. It is free of fins and vertical body sides, the main surfaces are highly oblique to the angles from which it is most likely to be illuminated, and the engines are—again, by virtue of the basic design—buried within the wings. Because the main purpose of the flying wing was to achieve lower drag, the Horten aircraft were designed to carry all their fuel and weapons internally.

John K. "Jack" Northrop, the founder and technical leader of the California company that bore his name, also realized that his flying wings would be less detectable than bombers of conventional configuration. The XB-35's metal propellers would have confounded any efforts at RCS reduction, but its jet-powered derivative, the YB-49, was different. Northrop promoted its reduced radar detectability as a significant advantage, in 1948 carrying out demonstration flights against coastal radar stations.

Northrop had not developed the flying wing because of its low observables characteristics, but because he believed in its aerodynamic and structural advantages. The flying wing's reduced detectability was a serendipitous benefit.

The reverse case applied when Northrop designers approached the requirement for a new bomber in the late seventies. They had Stealth uppermost in their minds, but the B-2 is nonetheless closer to the ideal of an all-wing airplane than any aircraft since the YB-49.

Flying wings and their advocates have existed as long as the airplane itself. In Great Britain, J. W. Dunne flew a tailless aircraft in 1909. The German designer Hugo Junkers, however, was the first to conceive of a true flying wing or all-wing aircraft. The payload, the crew, the fuel, and the engines would be accommodated inside a large, thick wing. To those who followed in Junkers' tracks, the flying wing was no less than the ideal shape for an airplane.

The conventional airplane has a wing to lift it and two tail surfaces to stabilize and control it. In early airplanes, the fuselage was a simple frame that held the tail at a distance from the wing and gave it enough leverage to do its job; later, the frame was skinned over and used to accommodate the airplane's load.

Both Northrop and the Hortens saw the benefits of flying wings in the same way. The fuselage and tail assembly represented weight and drag. The fin and tailplane provided neither lift nor useful space. In a conventional aircraft, drag was also caused by aerodynamic interference between both the wing and the fuselage and the fuselage and tail surfaces.

The flying wing was structurally efficient. The wing of a conventional aircraft is like a beam with a heavy weight—the body—hung at its midpoint. The wing produces lift along its span, so the weight in the middle will bend the beam downwards. In a flying wing, however, the mass of the aircraft is spread evenly along the wingspan, so the bending loads are much smaller and the wing can be lighter.

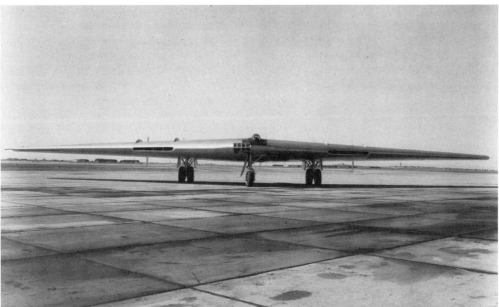

The wingspans of the B-2 and the YB-49 are identical to the foot. However, the front view shows that the B-2 is much deeper in section than the YB-49; in fact, it is almost seventy-five per cent heavier. Northrop, Bill Sweetman

According to Northrop, the flying wing would have less drag than the conventional aircraft of the same weight. It would cruise faster on less power, so it would need less fuel to attain a given range, and could carry more payload. Northrop's XB-35 was designed to equal the warload and range of the Convair B-36, but with two thirds the gross weight and two thirds the power.

The problem was that, while flying wings offer performance improvements, they pose problems, and the tools to solve some of these were not available in the forties. Stability and control were the biggest challenges. It was a rare airplane in those days that did not undergo some sort of redesign to its tail surfaces during development; to solve a handling problem, designers would make small changes to the size and shape of the tail surfaces.

A flying wing is different: its behavior about all three axes tends to be coupled (a movement in yaw tends to result in a movement in pitch), and there are no tail surfaces to provide a quick fix. It is amazing that the big Northrop wings flew as well as they did, with first-generation power-boosted flight controls (specially developed by Northrop) and no modern electronics.

The YB-49 did not meet USAF handling requirements, because it took too long for the pilot to level out for a bombing run; however, late in the test program, Northrop fitted the aircraft with a Minneapolis-Honeywell invention, a device that detected and automatically corrected the aircraft's motions in yaw. It was called a stability augmentation system (SAS) and was the forerunner of today's fly-by-wire (FBW) flight control systems.

Jet speeds were another problem for the flying wing. Just below the speed of sound, supersonic shock waves begin to form above an aircraft's wing. At the time, the only way to delay such phenomena to jet speeds was to make the wing thinner, but this militated against the whole object of the flying wing design, because it prevented components from being built into the wing. High-speed stability was also a problem. Northrop's own X-4, designed to evaluate the high-speed behavior of tailless aircraft, showed a rapid reduction in stability above Mach 0.88.

Above all, it was the lack of a mission that kept the flying wing on the shelf during the fifties and sixties. Jack Northrop himself had noted in 1947 that the benefits of the flying wing were greatest when the configuration was close to an ideal, with everything inside the wing. This is difficult for a small aircraft such as a fighter. It is also hard to achieve on a cargo aircraft, because its loads are so large that only a vast flying wing can accommodate them. The bomber, a large aircraft with small, dense payloads, is the most suitable candidate for an all-wing configuration. The trouble was that, from 1954 until 1978, SAC wanted supersonic bombers.

In the early seventies, however, flying wing designs started to reappear, because advances in the state of the art promised to solve many of its problems. Stability and control were an example. From the early SAS tested on the YB-49 had stemmed a line of more sophisticated devices, designed to tame the behavior of supersonic aircraft by sensing and counteracting any divergence before it could endanger the aircraft, and with multiple channels so that no single failure could cause a crash.

Next, designers realized that the multi-channel SAS could be mated with another new technology—the use of electronic signals, rather than steel cables or rods—to control the hydraulic

This view emphasizes the height and width of the dorsal hump behind the cockpit. The hump accommodates avionics, but its shape is driven by the need to blend the cockpit into *the wing without any breaks in the contours. A smaller hump would have meant a flatter cockpit with poor visibility.* Bill Sweetman

actuators that move the airplane's control surfaces. The advantages of FBW systems is that they are very responsive and can adjust the controls many times a second. Unlike the earlier stab-aug systems, they can stabilize an aircraft during a dynamic maneuver rather than limiting its excursions from a constant flight path.

Because of this, an FBW aircraft need not be naturally stable. This technology was first applied to such fighters as the F-16 and F-18, making them lighter and more maneuverable, but is now used even on airliners such as the A320.

For the flying wing, FBW permits the elimination of even the small vertical surfaces found on the YB-49: a tremendous breakthrough in all-aspect RCS reduction. Also, because the system is so responsive, it can cause the controls to react as soon as the aircraft hits an air gust. Rather than absorbing the shocks imposed by rough air in its structure, the aircraft actively resists it through the control system. The aircraft can be lighter (the structure does not have to be

as strong) and will ride more smoothly, particularly at low level.

Time has also dealt with the high-speed problems. In the seventies, faster computers made it possible to model the complex transonic airflows over a wing in three dimensions, instead of treating them as a series of slices. The advancing technology was visible in the wings of jet airliners: from one generation to the next, they became deeper at the tips, changed section to a much greater extent along the span, and became much thicker at the root. The new wings had lower drag, were lighter, and could store more fuel than the wings of the earlier generation of aircraft. All this technology could be applied to the B-2.

The aircraft that emerged from the Palmdale hangar in November 1988, therefore, was not just a revival of the flying wing, but a new interpretation of the concept in the light of current aviation technology.

The B-2's basic shape was determined by payload and range requirements, the need to accommodate all of the components, weapons, and fuel inside the wing, and the overriding demands of stability, control, and low observables. Payload and range set a lower limit to the span. The leading edge sweep angle was determined by the desired high-subsonic cruising speed and by the need to locate the aerodynamic center close to the center of gravity.

The length of the centerbody section was determined by depth: it had to be deep enough to accommodate a normal cockpit and the weapon bays, which meant that it had to have a minimum length to avoid excessive drag. Outboard of the centerbody section, the chord was set by the need to integrate the engines and their low observable inlet and exhaust systems into the wing. A benefit of the broad center-section was that it was easier to design it with the gentle slopes demanded by Stealth.

Although the chord close to the centerline had to be long, Northrop designers knew the planform area of a flying wing sets its weight and drag. As a result, the Advanced Technology Bomber (ATB) design emerged with a long, deep centerbody section, blended into thinner and more slender outer wings. The centerbody section provided volume; the outer wings carried the control surfaces and provided stability and span for low drag. Overall, the shape had less area and less weight and drag than a simpler triangle or delta.

Aerodynamically and structurally, the lift distribution was not what it would be in an ideal flying wing, but the basic performance was still high; because of the wing's great span and the elimination of the tail and body, the aerodynamic efficiency of the ATB was close to that of the Lockheed U-2, a very

AV-1 and AV-2 at Edwards Air Force Base during 1991. The dark tone of the wingtips *and leading edges indicates the presence of radar-absorbent material.* Northrop

AV-1 taxis at low power at Palmdale, before its first flight. The shortness of the body—as deep as a B-52 fuselage but little longer than an *F-15—is evident. The hawk's-beak nose shape satisfies the conflicting demands of Stealth and aerodynamics.* USAF

specialized aircraft with a much smaller design envelope. As a result, the ATB would be lighter than the B-1, but would carry more weapons over a greater distance; and its warload and range performance would be in the same class as the B-52, which is fifty tons heavier and requires almost twice as much power.

The original ATB design was very similar to Markarian's first sketches, with only one trailing-edge kink at midspan. In 1983, however, the aircraft was redesigned, delaying the program by a year. The change resulted from a "known unknown." The B-2 had always been intended as an all-altitude aircraft capable of low-level penetration. Initially, Northrop planned the aircraft to fly at Mach 0.55 at low altitude (about the same as the B-52), but, as the competition entered its final stages, it became clear that the bomber would have enough power (because of its low drag) to reach Mach 0.8.

Northrop adjusted its final offer to reflect this, while cautioning the USAF

that it had not had time to fully model the aeroelastic effects of the higher loads and more rigid structure. As it turned out, the design needed much more elevon area to control its response to low-level gusts, and some of the elevon area needed to be located at a more rigid point on the wing.

To provide the extra elevon space, the intermediate wing section (between the landing gear bays and the slender outer wing) was extended outwards and backwards, creating the B-2's characteristic saw-toothed trailing edge, but making the intermediate wing longer, deeper, and stiffer. To offset the resulting increase in area, weight, and drag, the outer wings were made shorter and more slender.

At the same time, the bomber was redesigned internally, so that more of the loads would be carried through large structural beams inside the body, rather than being distributed all through the skin. In the process, the inlets were moved aft and the cockpit was moved forwards. Overall, the result was a stronger, more durable aircraft with better ride characteristics at low level.

The new aerodynamic tools that improved the design of transonic wings have made it possible to design the centerbody, which is little longer than the fuselage of an F-15 and has the same depth as a B-52 fuselage. This makes it possible to locate two large weapon bays side by side between the engine bays. Each bay contains either a Boeing-developed Advanced Applications Rotary Launcher (AARL), capable of carrying eight large weapons, such as B83 free-fall nuclear bombs or guided conventional weapons, or a "stack" system for carrying smaller conventional weapons.

The crew compartment is reached through a ventral hatch to the left of the nosewheel bay. The central hummock behind the cockpit contains much of the avionics system. It is considerably wider than it would have to be if it were simply a fairing behind the cockpit. The B-2's cockpit windows are huge, so large that they throw the aircraft out of proportion and make it look smaller than it is. They are large for the same reason that the cockpit windows of a DC-10 are large: a cockpit window has to provide the pilot with a given angular field of view, and the further the window is from the pilot's seat, the bigger it has to be. Comparing the location of the ejection-seat hatches with the width of the dorsal hump shows how wide and high the latter is.

The engines, outboard of the weapon bays, are buried completely within the wing. The raised structures behind the inlets, which looked like engine nacelles in the first USAF impression, are simply fairings. The S-shaped inlet ducts curve down to the engines, which are accessible from below the aircraft. The exhaust ducts flatten out to wide slits and open into overwing trenches.

B-2 Flight Controls

The B-2's aerodynamic characteristics are unique. Compared with a normal design of the same weight, the B-2 has much more span and wing area, so

AV-1 rolls out for its first takeoff. The trailing edge surfaces, which drooped when the aircraft was static, are beginning to move into flight position. (The system was later mod- *ified so that these surfaces remain in trail at all speeds.) Visible here is the complex shape of the leading edge.* USAF

July 17, 1989: the B-2 rotates and leaves the ground with minimal stick pressure or elevon deflection. The wingtip brake-rudders are "cracked five and five": on both sides, the upper section is set 5deg up and the lower section 5deg down. At low speeds, this sharpens the B-2's yaw response, because the rudders do not have to penetrate a "dead zone" of slipstream from the wing before they take effect. USAF

the lift coefficient (a measure of how much lift must be produced by each square foot of wing) does not have to be as high. While conventional aircraft of similar performance have complex flaps and other devices to raise the lift coefficient for takeoff and landing, the B-2 needs none and usually lifts off at a conservative 140 knots.

The B-2 operates over a smaller angle of attack (alpha) range than a conventional aircraft—again, because of its big wing—and flies in a fairly flat, constant attitude, regardless of speed and weight. The force that the control surfaces need to generate to trim or balance the aircraft is, therefore, fairly small, and the drag that results from this force is minimal.

In most respects, the B-2 is close to neutrally stable. If it had conventional controls, which moved in exact accordance with the pilot's stick and rudder movements, any disturbance would tend to push the aircraft on to a new flight-

path. It would not diverge farther from its original path unless it was disturbed again, but it would require an action by the pilot to resume its former attitude and speed.

However, the B-2 does not have conventional controls; it has an FBW system with four separate channels. Even after one channel has failed, three channels remain operational. If a second channel fails, the system's logic will detect that it is functioning differently from the two healthy channels and will shut it down. The system gets information about the airplane's speed and attitude from a Rosemount air-data system that relies on flush ports rather than probes. The ports are installed in sets of four, one for each channel.

The FBW system drives nine very large control surfaces occupying the entire trailing edge, apart from the area behind the engines. The outermost pair of surfaces are split horizontally and operate both symmetrically, as speed-brakes, and asymmetrically, as rudders. The flattened, pointed tail of the centerbody—known as the gust load alleviation system (GLAS), or the beavertail—is an elevator. The remaining six surfaces are elevons for pitch and roll control.

Many aircraft have no horizontal tail, but the absence of a vertical fin is one of the B-2's unique features. B-2 designer Irv Waaland describes a conventional aircraft without a vertical fin as "like an arrow without feathers." The flying wing is different, because it is short from front to rear and has no features to generate destabilizing side forces. "The all-wing design is neutrally stable directionally," Waaland says. "All you need is adequate control." The same characteristic of the flying wing also makes the aircraft more stable at low altitudes, because gusts do not disturb it in yaw.

Pilots describe the B-2 as a pleasant aircraft to fly. It is not a fighter; its flying wing design limits it to a relatively small alpha range, its long wingspan pre-cludes a rapid roll rate, and it does not have the thrust for high-g maneuvering or rapid acceleration. It is, however, more responsive than most large aircraft, because the flight-control system (FCS) is powerful and the airframe is stiff. Because of its low drag, it out-accelerates most aircraft of its size, and the fighter-type engines respond quickly to throttle inputs.

Before the B-2 flew, many critics expected the aircraft to be only marginally stable. Even on the first flight, however, observers noted the B-2's almost unnatural steadiness on final approach, with absolutely no visible wing rock or "hunting" in alpha. The entire in-flight refueling envelope was cleared in a single flight, a first-time achievement for a brand-new aircraft.

The FCS normally keeps the B-2 at zero beta (that is to say, with no sideslip or crab) and a constant alpha, selected by the pilot. At low level and high speeds, the constant-alpha law tends to counter-act wind gusts immediately: an upward gust increases the aircraft's alpha, and

The B-2 is one of few large subsonic aircraft with no wing flaps. Its great span and wing area, however, give it a similar field perfor-mance to that of a Boeing 727, a commercial jet roughly half its size. USAF

Superb view of AV-1 as it passes over the Palmdale fence on its first flight. The massive weapon bays, with more usable volume than the bigger B-52, are clearly visible, as are the engine access doors. Note also the complex camber of the leading edge. Doug Sheridan/Wide World

AV-1 flexes its controls for the first time above the California desert. Drag rudders and elevons are deflected to reverse its right-hand turn, and the central elevator is pitching the aircraft down. USAF

so the FCS commands the aircraft to pitch down. At the same time, the abrupt alpha increase is detected by the gust-alleviation laws in the FCS, which signals the elevons and beavertail to apply more nose-up trim on the outer wings and less on the centerline. This reduces the peak bending moment. The ride quality is not quite as good as that of the B-1—there is no substitute for very high-wing loading—but is much better than a B-52's.

The B-2 aerodynamic design was primarily based on computational fluid dynamics (CFD), according to aerodynamicist Hans Grellmann, although CFD for whole-airframe design was in its infancy when the program started. "We had to make do with tools that were never designed to do the job," Grellmann says. A transonic wing analysis code was adapted to define the entire wing. CFD could not directly account for engine flows, so the aerodynamics team subtracted the engine flow from their calculations, leaving only the spilling airflow. CFD was also used to investigate important handling areas, such as in-flight refueling and behavior in ground effect. "We relied on CFD, and used the wind tunnel to tell us that our codes were valid," says Grellmann.

Several tunnel models—all produced by numerically controlled machines, driven from the same computer database that was used in the production of the full-size aircraft—were used for more than 24,000 hours of total tunnel time. The "workhorse" was a sting-mounted force and moment model with working inlets. The airloads model was similar. Several models were dedicated to inlet tests. The total effect of aerodynamic, inlet, and exhaust flows in the centerbody section was simulated by an afterbody and jet effects model.

Detail design challenges included the need to push the thickness of the centerbody section to the limit of flow separation, to accommodate a body depth equal to that of the B-52 in the bomber's 69-foot overall length. The aircraft was also to have conventional pitch and stalling characteristics, despite a low observables design group that wanted the leading edge to be as sharp as possible. The high degree of twist and drastic leading edge camber variation visible on the B-2 evolved as a complex compromise between aerodynamics and Stealth.

Stealth Engines

The B-2 is powered by four General Electric F118-GE-100 engines. The F118 is a member of a phenomenally successful family that includes the B-1's F101 engine; the F110 fighter engine, which powers some F-16s and the latest F-14s; and the CFM56, the world's best-selling commercial engine. The F118 is, basically, an F110 without an afterburner but with a more efficient fan that provides more power.

The F110 was developed from the B-1 engine, the F101, by fitting a smaller low-pressure spool and thereby reducing the bypass ratio from 2:1 to 0.87:1. The result was a slightly slimmer and lighter engine that would fit in a fighter, but would use more fuel at subsonic speed. Why choose a fighter engine for the B-2 when a more efficient engine was not only available but in service with SAC?

The answer is that the biggest problem in propulsion for a Stealth aircraft is the design of the inlets, which have to conceal the highly visible first stage of the engine from radar while supplying it efficiently with air. The F101 is a more efficient engine than the F110, considered in isolation, but it needs more air than the F110 and its larger fan is a bigger radar target. It would, therefore, require a bigger, more complex inlet to meet Stealth objectives, and its performance advantage would be wiped out or reversed.

The first Stealth aircraft, the Lockheed Have Blue and F-117A, used straight inlet ducts behind faceted grilles treated with special radar-absorbent material (RAM). Northrop designers wanted to avoid these grilles, because they cause thrust losses and icing problems. Instead, the B-2 inlets were mounted over the wings (where radars beneath the aircraft could not see into them) and curved to block the line of sight between the inlet mouth and the engine face. The curve had to be quite sharp, because the flying wing shape did not leave more than a minimum amount of room for the complete inlet, engine, and exhaust.

The inlets take the form of S-ducts, which project through the upper skin of the wing. Shallow secondary scoops, built into the wing just ahead of the main inlets, swallow the turbulent air next to the wing surface before it can disrupt flow in the duct. The inlets' complex shape results from the interaction between the curvature of the seam-less skin and the alignment of the inlet lips with the outer edges of the aircraft.

The integration of the engines into the wing was one of the riskiest areas in the whole design. The need to conceal the engines from detection by radar meant that the inlets had to be above the wing, which, aerodynamically, is the most difficult of all locations.

Although the B-2 is a subsonic aircraft, its thick supercritical wing sections accelerate the air to supersonic speeds over the wing. The inlet region resembles two supercritical wing sections in series. The first is the area behind the leading edge, where the airflow accelerates to supersonic speed and is then recompressed to subsonic speed before being swallowed by the main inlet and the auxiliary boundary-layer scoop. The second supercritical section comprises the region from the inlet lip to the exhaust exit, where the flow is accelerated and recompressed once again. In cruising flight, the inlet is spilling air (as most inlets do) and the interaction with the flow over the wing translates all the way to the wingtip. Because of this, it was impossible to predict or test the B-2's aerodynamic performance without taking the propulsion system into account.

In the early days of the program, Northrop built a full-scale replica of the inlet, complete with two engines, and tested it on the ground. Only one serious problem turned up: a certain amount of flow separation in the tightly curved duct, leading to a loss of power at low speeds. The solution was to add retractable auxiliary inlet scoops above the wing, and these were fitted to the first two B-2s. In the real aircraft, however, the problem proved to be less severe, and the scoops have been deleted from later aircraft.

Walkway markings over the B-2's wings are located over major structural beams and joints, avoiding risk of damage to the smooth surface. The walkway lines outboard of the engines outline the junction of the intermediate and outer wings. USAF

Stealth Materials and Construction

Structurally, the B-2 consists of six major assemblies. The center wing assembly, built by Boeing, contains the weapon bays and the avionics bays above and behind them. In front of this is the crew station assembly, produced by Northrop. On either side are the two very complex intermediate wing assemblies, produced by LTV, that house the inlets, exhausts, engine bays, and main landing gear bays. The two 70-foot outer wings are also produced by Boeing, as are the weapon launchers and landing gear.

The components of the B-2 built by Northrop are only a small proportion of the total weight. They consist of the cockpit and the entire perimeter of the aircraft: the leading edges, wingtips, control surfaces, and fixed trailing edge structure. For Northrop, this makes good business sense. Much of the value of a contract is in the design, the integration (which includes the cockpit), and the use of company-proprietary technology; in a Stealth aircraft, the edges are very important.

Inside the center and intermediate wing sections are two very large titanium carry-through box (CTB) structures, one behind the cockpit and the other one aft of the engine bay. Otherwise, the primary structural material is a carbon fiber and epoxy composite. Also known as graphite-epoxy, it consists of nearly pure carbon fibers, which have an extremely high tensile strength, held in a matrix of epoxy resin. Resin-impregnated carbon-fiber fabric (pre-preg) in the form of sheets or tapes is laid-up to form components, which are then heated under pressure in an autoclave, permanently setting the resin and bonding the layers into a solid part. The B-2 includes many of the largest carbon-fiber parts ever made, including centerbody section skins that are more than one inch thick and spars and skins more than seventy feet long.

Carbon fiber is lighter than metal for equivalent strength and improves the performance of the B-2, but one of the most important reasons for choosing the new material had to do with Stealth.

The frame above the tail of AV-1 carries a trailing air-data sensor, included on early flights to validate the stealthy air-data system installed on all B-2s. USAF

Carbon fiber is less dense than metal, so carbon-fiber skins are thicker than metal skins of the same strength, and composite parts can be assembled by "co-curing" them: autoclaving them together, so that the parts bond together with a strength equal to that of the original material.

The thick, fastener-free skins produced by this method are smoother and more stable than riveted metal skins. This is important, because a smooth surface—to be maintained for twenty years or longer—was critical to Northrop's Stealth design technique.

The structural design was more difficult than expected. The skin had to be made thicker and heavier than predicted because its Stealth characteristics might be compromised if it buckled under loads. Other requirements cost money, Waaland said later: "We entered the program with what we thought was a full range of validated materials, both low-observable and non-low-observable.

Northrop added heat and vibration sensors above the exhausts (white lines) on early flights. The "decks" aft of the exhaust have been a design problem. USAF

We were required to validate our materials for nuclear flash and dust, long-life ultra-violet exposure, rain, supportability, producibility and a lot of other concerns. The bottom line is that nothing that we started with survived." In many cases, new materials not only cost money to develop, but were more expensive in production as well.

The details of the shape that make the B-2 look so strange—the rectilinear plan-view and the curvaceous elevations—have little to do with aerodynamics and a great deal to do with Stealth, particularly in the radar spectrum.

The B-2 posed new challenges in Stealth, because its mission was to penetrate into a deep, internetted air defense system. The result was that a radar behind the B-2, or hundreds of miles to the side of it, could be as dangerous as one in front of it, because it could still be used to cue a SAM system or a fighter. All-aspect Stealth was of the essence.

When Stealth was first discussed, the tendency was to assume that Stealth aircraft would have curved exteriors. This, however, is only half right. A constant curve is an "isotropic scatterer"; it reflects equally in all directions, an effect that has been likened to the rear window of a Volkswagen Beetle, gleaming in the sun.

As noted earlier, Lockheed achieved Stealth by using only flat surfaces; Northrop went in the opposite direction. The B-2's curves constantly change radius, as though they are sections of a spiral, rather than arcs of a circle. The company describes the upper and lower surfaces as "seamless"; there is not a crease in sight.

The B-2 shape is the result of two principles: all surfaces are oblique to any likely radar beam; and, rather than aligning crease or fold lines away from the main illumination angles, creases have been eliminated. That is simple enough to say, but in fact, the process of designing an aircraft so that its exterior shape is in complete accordance with the principles of electromagnetic scattering as well as the laws of aerodynamics is almost unbelievably complex and could not have been attempted before the advent of supercomputers.

However, this principle could not be applied to the leading and trailing edges of the wing and the inlets. If these were infinitely sharp, they would be invisible to radar, but structural and aerodynamic laws dictate that the edges of the aircraft will have a measurably curved

radius. The result is that there will be a reflection from the edge.

Edge reflections cannot be eliminated, so they are managed according to three principles. The first is to angle all the edges as sharply as possible away from the most important illumination angle—that is, from about the same level and predominantly in front of the aircraft. This was a factor in setting the B-2's leading-edge sweep angle.

The second principle of edge management is to avoid inside corners, which distort the electromagnetic field along the edges. Although inside corners cannot be eliminated, they can be reduced in number and located on the back

The dark band around the leading edge and wingtips consists of deep, effective radar-absorbent structure (RAS). Because of the B-2's configuration, the RAS will be effective against radars illuminating it from up to 90deg off the nose. The white line visible behind the bomber is the towline for the trailing air-data sensor. USAF

of the aircraft, where they are tactically less important. The most visible edges, in the front, are ruler straight, from nose to wing tip.

The third principle is to align all the edges along the smallest possible number of vectors. Edge reflections, like surface reflections, are strongest when the radar beam is at right angles to the edge. Also, radar detection range is determined by the strongest reflection, not by the total of large and small reflections. A small reflection—from an access door, for example—can be concealed under a larger one on the same bearing, if the edge of the access door is parallel to the larger edge. The reflection from the access door has, effectively, been eliminated. On the B-2, the weapon-bay doors, landing gear doors, crew access

Weapons bays, engine bays, and landing gear bays occupy much of the B-2's smooth lower skin. The dark patch beneath the leading edge is one of the two flush antenna bays for the APQ-181 radar. USAF

hatch, and many other apertures conform to this principle.

Because access panels have to be treated so carefully, it is best to eliminate as many of them as possible. This involves careful design. On the B-2, one panel usually gives access to several systems; other subsystems, such as the avionics, are installed so that they can be reached through existing apertures, such as the crew boarding hatch, weapon bays, and landing gear bays. Actually, designers have discovered this to be a better layout, from the maintenance viewpoint, than providing a host of access panels.

Shape is by far the biggest factor in reducing RCS, but special RAM is necessary to mop up residual scattering from the shaped surfaces and to suppress reflections from features such as edges and inlets, which cannot be totally stealthy in their basic design. RAM is applied to an existing structure and adds to its weight without increasing its strength; radar-absorbing structure (RAS) involves building these materials into load-bearing structure.

All RAM and RAS work on the same basic principle. Radar signals bounce efficiently off of any conductive object, but some substances reflect radar waves efficiently and others do not. The difference is in the substance's molecular structure. Some materials include free electrons in their molecular chains; electrical engineers call them "lossy."

Radars, like radios and televisions, operate on a given wavelength; in the case of most radars, the wavelength is measured in gigahertz (GHz), or billions of cycles per second. When a radar transmitter illuminates an object made of a lossy material, the free electrons oscillate at the frequency of the radar wave, absorbing some of the radar energy. But these particles have friction and inertia,

Where'd he go? Visual Stealth is inherent in the flying-wing design, with no vertical fin and no high-contrast vertical sides. Chase, tanker, and photo pilots report that they often find the B-2 by looking for the F-16 chase plane. USAF

however tiny, and some of the radar's energy is transformed into a virtually immeasurable amount of heat energy. These substances are "lossy dielectrics" because they are non-conductive.

Other absorbent materials, including iron compounds called ferrites are known as "lossy magnetics." A radar wave induces a magnetic field in the ferrite material, but the field must switch polarity at the radar frequency; this process is not 100 per cent efficient, and much of the radar energy is absorbed and transformed into heat.

Most of these lossy materials have little or no strength or toughness. But many materials, including glass, ceramics, and many plastics, are simply "dielectric": they do not conduct electricity, and radar waves pass straight through them with minimal reflection or absorption—but they are strong enough to use in aircraft structures.

RAM, therefore, usually consists of a lossy ingredient—a dielectric, such as carbon, or a magnetic ferrite—which is molded into a dielectric matrix, usually a polymer of some kind. Lockheed developed a lossy plastic material for the A-12, and a ferrite-based paint known as "iron ball" is used on the SR-71. The F-117 was originally covered in flexible RAM, resembling floor tiles in thickness and weight, but is now coated with a sprayed-on RAM.

Some basic limitations apply to all kinds of RAM. All of them absorb a portion of the radar energy and reflect the rest. A given type of RAM is also most effective at a certain frequency and less so at others. Similarly, the effectiveness of RAM varies with the angle of the incident radar wave. Generally, too, the thickness and weight of RAM increase with its effectiveness.

RAM is also formulated and applied so that the small reflection from the front face of the absorber is cancelled by a residual reflection from the structure beneath it. The basic technique is to make the total pathway of energy within the RAM equal to half a wavelength, so that the residual reflection is exactly out-of-phase with the front-face reflection. The RAM can be much thinner than the nominal wavelength of the radar and still achieve cancellation, because the wavelength inside the material is much shorter than it is in free space.

Solid RAM coatings cover a frequency range of about 20:1. This is enough to address air-to-air and surface-to-air missile radars (from the L band up to the Ku band) but more elaborate schemes are used to cover the full radar spectrum, which includes VHF radars with wavelengths of almost two meters.

The task is complicated by the fact that different radars affect the target in different ways. According to Lockheed scientist Dr. Vaughn Cable: "High frequencies have the same effect that you see when you shine a flashlight down the street and see a cat's eyes flash. At low frequencies, we consider radar as hammering the target and leaving the target in a mode that rings. It's a resonance effect."

Alan Brown, designer of the F-117, compares a typical wide-band RAS, used on the edges of a stealth aircraft, to "a stereo system, with a tweeter and a woofer." The "tweeter" is a high-frequency ferromagnetic absorber, applied over a resistive layer that reflects higher frequencies but allows low-frequency signals to pass through.

Deceptively small from many angles, the B-2 weighs as much as a Boeing 767 jetliner, and its wingspan is greater than the USAF's big KC-10 tanker. USAF

Beneath this resistive layer is the low-frequency "woofer": a glass-fiber honeycomb core, treated from front to back with a steadily increasing amount of resistant material. Brown calls it "an electromagnetic shock absorber. It's very soft in front, but we still absorb pretty much all the energy inside, because we don't want the energy to hit the vertical front face of the structure." Although from a Lockheed source, this is probably an accurate description of how the B-2's leading edges are built.

The advantage of honeycomb RAS is depth without proportionate weight. A honeycomb RAS might consist of an outer skin of Kevlar 149 and epoxy composite, which is transparent to radar, and an inner skin of reflective graphite and epoxy. The Nomex core, between them, would be treated with an absor-

bent agent, increasing in density from front to rear of the honeycomb.

The front-face reflection of such an RAS would be minimal. As the radar wave encounters the thinly spread absorber on the outer edges of the core, a small part of its energy is absorbed and another small part is scattered. As the wave proceeds through the core, it encounters more densely loaded core material which both absorbs and reflects more energy. But before the reflected energy can reach free space again, it is once more attenuated by the outermost layer of absorber.

The use of RAM and RAS is dictated by shape and the likely positions of radars that will illuminate the aircraft. On the B-2, RAM is used inside the inlets and around the exhausts, which cannot be designed in full accordance

Only one flight was required to clear the B-2's entire refueling envelope behind the KC-10. With its stiff airframe and fly-by-wire con- *trols, the B-2 is much easier to handle than the demanding B-52. USAF*

with Stealth shaping laws, and around the edges of doors. The largest RAS structures are the leading edges, which are most exposed to long-range, low-frequency early warning radars. The only possible drawback of the B-2's flying wing design is that it implies a deep, moderately swept leading edge. This in turn means that the design relies to a great extent on RAS to defeat such radars.

Logically, the honeycomb RAS is placed on the part of the airframe that is most likely to reflect radar at tactically significant distances: the leading edges. The B-2 also seems to use non-structural RAM, with a radar-absorbent paint coating, on its wing leading edges

and wingtips, inside its air inlets, and around its exhausts.

The design of the engine exhausts is the primary battlefield in the war against IR detection. There are many types of IR sensors in service, and their different capabilities are sometimes confused. The basic fact is that the atmosphere absorbs IR energy. At a range of a few miles, a small IR sensor can receive enough energy to produce a TV-type image of the scene, but at greater ranges, this capability is much diminished.

Most medium-to-long-range systems, such as the IR search and track systems (IRSTS) fitted to Soviet interceptors and the homing heads of IR-

Refueling from the KC-135 is also possible, if a little more difficult. Like the C-5, the B-2 generates a bow wave from its broad nose that pushes up on the smaller tanker's tail and causes it to pitch down. The tanker pilots call it "surfing." USAF

guided missiles, do not detect the IR emissions from the aircraft itself, but the radiation from the hot air and water vapor emitted by its engines.

Infrared Stealth

The B-2's exhausts are built into the top of the wing. The primary nozzles are well ahead of the trailing edge and lead into a pair of soft-lipped trenches, lined with heat-resistant tiles, which flare outwards. The key to degrading the performance of an IRSTS is to ensure that the exhaust dissipates as quickly as possible after leaving the aircraft. To this end, the engines are fitted with flow mixers to blend the cold bypass air with the hot air that passes through the combustor and the turbine, and the considerable amount of cold boundary layer swallowed by the secondary inlets is injected into the exhaust stream to cool it further.

The exhausts are wide and flat, rather than round; the perimeter of the exhaust is longer than the perimeter of a round exhaust stream, and mixing takes place more quickly. The exhaust cavities are actually invisible from directly behind the aircraft. As the exhaust passes over the trenches, it is bent back into the desired direction by the Coanda effect, which causes the flow to adhere to the trench surface. Finally, the interaction between the exhaust stream and the airflow over the aircraft, at each angled side of the exhaust "trench," creates a vortex that further promotes mixing.

Acoustic, smoke, and contrail signatures also mainly affect the design of the propulsion system. In the acoustic area, the main challenge is, perhaps, the possibility that an adversary could install an interlinked chain of highly sensitive microphones. An engine installation such as the B-2's, with a sinuous inlet and an exhaust mixer, however, is likely

to be naturally quiet. Reducing visible smoke is largely a matter of efficient design in the combustion section of the engine.

Contrail control is a different problem. As long ago as the fifties, the USAF experimented with systems that in-

The B-2 refueling receptacle rotates around its longitudinal axis, like that of the F-117. It has to close tightly and reliably to maintain the bomber's Stealth characteristics. Note the ejection hatch for the third crew member, on the right side of the aircraft, and the tactical commander's clipboard, resting in the massive space between the oversized windshield and the instrument panel. USAF

jected a chemical, chloro-fluoro-sulfonic acid, into the exhaust system. The effect of the chemical was to break down the water molecules in the exhaust to a size below the wavelength of white light, making them invisible. The chemical was highly corrosive, and a better system may well have been found for the B-2.

B-2 Performance

The B-2 was not designed to achieve a great advance in performance over the B-52. The Boeing bomber has a large enough range to perform the USAF's intended bomber missions, and its payload is large enough to accommodate as many nuclear weapons as could be realistically targeted in a single mission. Because the B-2 is more efficient, however, it is almost twenty-five per cent smaller than the B-52, and it uses much less fuel; this means that it can accomplish the same mission with less or no tanker support.

The great advance, of course, is in Stealth. The combination of the flying wing shape, Northrop's low-RCS shaping laws, and RAM and RAS made it possible for Northrop to predict, back in

This boomer's-eye view of AV-1 shows a row of flush antenna apertures on the spine of the aircraft, probably for communications systems or for the APR-50 electronic surveillance system; the auxiliary air inlets behind the main intakes; the quadruple pressure ports for the air-data system; and the curved windshield-blowing slits. USAF

the early stages of the program, that the bomber would demonstrate a massive reduction in reflectivity, approaching three orders of magnitude. If a nominal target had an RCS of 10m², therefore, the B-2 would have an RCS of 0.01m², equivalent to that of a small bird. A radar with a range of 200 miles against the standard aircraft would not detect the B-2 until it was thirty-five miles away. RCS predictions were tested during the risk-reduction phase of the program, using large-scale models on Northrop's own range in the Tejon Pass, just above Edwards, and the USAF's huge RATSCAT facility in New Mexico. Early RCS tests with the first B-2, conducted in 1991, basically validated the RCS predictions.

B-2 Cockpit and Crew

In the early days of Stealth, there was some concern, even among professionals, that it might be difficult to build a stealthy aircraft without compromising its ability to find its targets. The F-117A, for instance, is basically intended to find fixed targets in clear air. The B-2 is designed to attack virtually any large surface target with no outside help, under any weather conditions, and this has driven the design of its avionics system.

The system is managed by the B-2's two-member crew. Both are rated pilots; the pilot occupies the left seat, and the mission commander sits on the right and has primary responsibility for navigation and weapon delivery. Behind the crew station is an area shared by avionics racks and space for a third crew station.

The cockpit is designed and equipped so that either crew member can perform the complete mission. Each pilot has four six-inch-square, full-color cathode-ray-tube (CRT) cockpit displays

arranged in a T shape, which show flight information, sensor inputs, or systems data on command. Each pilot also has a data entry panel to his right and a set of throttles to his left. (The throttles, like the flight controls, are linked electronically to the engines.) There is also a set of "master mode switches" that configure the displays and computers for preflight, take-off, cruise, and landing.

The third seat, well behind the pilots' seats, is partly a form of insurance. The B-1, designed in the seventies, has a crew of four: two pilots, an offensive systems operator (basically, a weapon aimer and navigator), and a defensive systems operator who runs the ECM system. Even with eighties'-technology displays and automation, halving the crew size on the B-2 was a risk, and the third station may have been retained in case the workload proved too great. As it was, more than 6,000 hours of manned simulation had been carried out before the B-2 was unveiled, convincing SAC that two pilots would be enough.

The radar-absorbent liner of the left inlet duct is just visible here. Northrop felt that lined S-ducts were preferable to gridded or baffled inlets. Bill Sweetman

Like many features of the B-2's shape, the profile of the central hummock results from tension between operational considerations and Stealth. In this case, visibility requirements set the depth and wrap-around angle of the windshield. Stealth dictated a minimum slope angle for the windshield panels and also ruled out a rapid flattening-out above the cockpit, resulting in a wide, high central fairing. Bill Sweetman

The two pilots are supported by the most comprehensive training system ever developed for a military aircraft. Historically, training devices and simulators have been developed once the aircraft has gone into production. In the case of the B-2, however, the USAF's premier training systems supplier, CAE-Link, has been a member of the prime contract team from the outset. The B-2 weapon system trainer (WST) is designed to simulate the entire combat mission. Its General Electric image-generating computers not only reproduce the out-the-window scene, but drive all the electronic cockpit displays from the same database. Other training devices will prepare the crew to take maximum advantage of their WST time.

Stealth Avionics and Radar

The avionics system that the crew must manage is the most sophisticated ever fitted to a combat aircraft and includes what is probably the world's most expensive airborne radar. It is intended to function with a high degree of reliability, with no outside help and

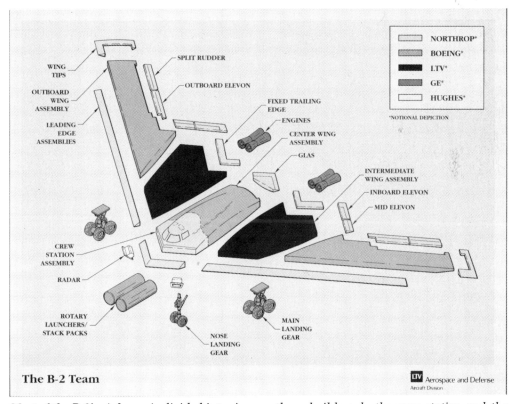

The B-2 Team

Most of the B-2's airframe is divided into six main components: the center wing, the crew station, and the intermediate and outboard wings on either side. Prime contractor Nor-throp builds only the crew station and the perimeter of the aircraft, which consists of radar-absorbing secondary structure and control surfaces. LTV

with the absolute minimum of tell-tale electronic emissions. Its primary functions are navigation and target detection.

The navigation subsystem (NSS) combines one of the newest navigation techniques with one of the oldest. It includes two units, either of which is capable of navigating the aircraft on its own, but is most accurate and reliable when working with the other. One of them is an inertial measurement unit (IMU) from Kearfott, basically similar to the inertial navigation systems originally developed for bombers and now used on most new commercial aircraft.

The other part of the NSS is a Northrop NAS-27 astro-inertial unit (AIU). Northrop pioneered this technology in the early fifties, when it developed the

Snark long-range cruise missile. Any inertial system drifts with time, because the system adds all movements from its starting point to derive its present position, and errors are therefore cumulative; when the Snark was designed, these drift rates were large enough to cause the weapon to miss its target. What was needed was a system that would, from time to time, fix the position of the missile precisely. The solution was a navigation system that found its way by the stars.

The AIU system developed for the Snark was based on a stabilized electro-optical telescope, capable of locking onto a pre-selected star even in cloudy daylight. A version of this system was used on the A-12 and SR-71, and an improved descendant is fitted to the B-2.

Early production-line photo shows three B-2s (the front one is probably AV-3), covered with protective white sheeting and black plastic mats to prevent surface marring. USAF

The B-2's APQ-181 radar (known as the radar subsystem, or RSS) was developed by the Radar Systems Group of Hughes Aircraft (part of General Motors). In the early days of the program, B-2 critics often complained that the bomber would have no way of finding its targets at long standoff ranges without betraying its presence by radar emissions. This argument was a measure of the effectiveness of the security protecting the development of low-probability-of-intercept (LPI) radar technology over many years.

Most LPI techniques are classified, but they include the adaptive management of power (the radar gradually increases its power until it can see a target and then holds its power level), the use of very-low-sidelobe antennas, and con-

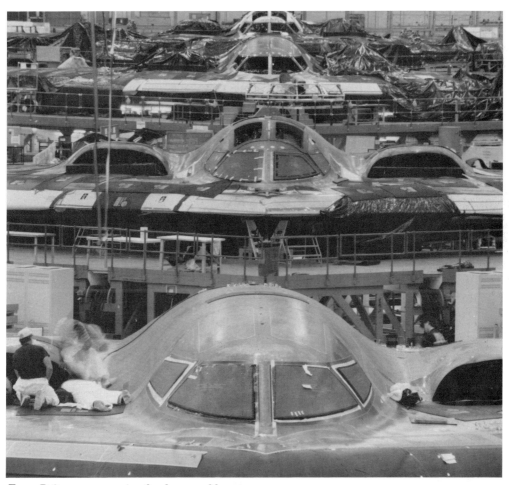

Four B-2s are seen in final assembly at Palmdale. The first aircraft has its RAM leading-edge installed. USAF

stant variations in frequency and waveform. The same fundamental fact that underlies the potential of LPI applies also to Stealth: because people have tended to assume as a matter of course that any radar transmission will be intercepted and classified, there was enormous room for improvement in terms of LPI.

The APQ-181 has two 585-pound antennas built into the lower leading edge of the wing, one on each side. Rather than moving physically, they are scanned electronically to steer the radar beam in azimuth and elevation. Each radar antenna has its own power supply, transmitter-receiver, and signal processing unit, and the two chains are cross-connected so that the radar can continue to perform even if part of one chain fails.

The radar operates in the Ku band (12-18 GHz), which is a higher frequency and shorter wavelength than the X-band (around 10 GHz) where most airborne radars operate. Ku-band radars suffer from more atmospheric absorption than X band and are less suitable for large-

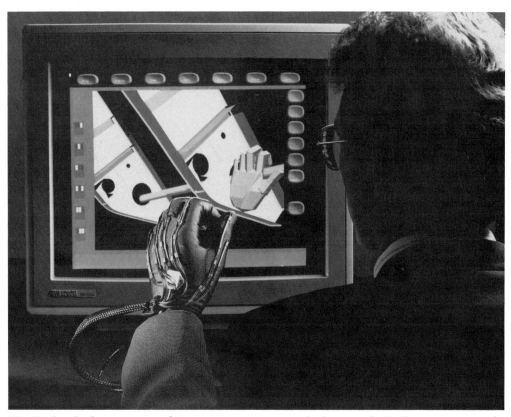

The B-2 has broken new ground in computer-integrated manufacturing. In an offshoot of the B-2 program, an engineer uses an instru-mented glove to check that a part can be assembled easily before it has been manufactured. Northrop

area searches because, all other things being equal, they require more power and more time to scan a given volume. They have inherently higher resolution than X-band radars, however, for a given antenna size, a Ku-band radar will have smaller and weaker sidelobes.

The radar's many modes include one for synthetic aperture radar (SAR), in which a target to one side of the flightpath is illuminated by many successive pulses as the aircraft moves. The signal processor can sum up the returns from each radar pulse and build up the image as though each pulse were received by a separate element in an extremely long array. Loral's APD-12, for example, is stated to achieve similar resolution to a "real" array 300 times as long as its own 66-inch antenna. With a combination of SAR, Ku band, and very high-speed processing, the APQ-181 should be capable of acquiring near-photographic imagery at a range of almost 100 miles from the B-2's cruising altitude.

Another likely mode is inverse SAR (ISAR), in which the measured movement of a target is used to build up radar imagery in the same way. ISAR was developed for maritime patrol aircraft, improving the resolution of their radars to the point where their crews could confidently classify ships at ranges of up to eighty miles.

The B-2 does not have a forward-looking-IR (FLIR) system, but the resolution of the radar is likely to be so high that it barely needs one. Moreover, FLIR is limited in range and ineffective in clouds or fog, whereas radar is not.

The radar is also used for terrain following and terrain avoidance (TF/TA) at low altitude, providing data to dual TF/TA processors that interface with the flight control system. In TF/TA mode, the radar images the terrain ahead of

The B-2 incorporates some of the largest advanced-composite components ever built. This giant autoclave was installed at LTV to cure composite parts under heat and pressure. LTV

the aircraft, measuring ground slope angles, detecting ridge-lines, and automatically steering the aircraft on a safe track. The navigation system uses stored terrain data, combined with the aircraft's known position, to map the terrain beyond the radar horizon and present that information to the crew.

Details of the B-2's electronic combat (EC) system, which includes components from IBM, Raytheon, Lockheed-Sanders, and Honeywell, are largely classified. However, it was revealed in 1991 that IBM supplies an EC subsystem designated as APR-50 for the B-2. The APR prefix indicates that the system is not merely designed to detect electronic emissions but to locate their source in both bearing and range.

USAF sources have consistently stressed that the B-2's defensive management subsystem (DMS) is passive:

This Boeing NKC-135A Flight Test Avionics Laboratory (FTAL) was modified to test the navigation and radar systems of the B-2, with a prototype APQ-181 radar antenna in the nose, a row of dorsal antennas, and the B-2's computers. By the time the B-2 made its first flight, the FTAL was already running as much software as a complete B-1. USAF

its primary function is to detect, identify, and locate emitters that present a threat to the aircraft, and to use other emissions to help the B-2's crew locate mobile targets. The key to making such a system work is a considerable amount of high-speed processing capacity and an effective antenna system, coupled with a very large database of known emitter locations.

A number of reports have referred to a B-2 electronic subsystem, built by Northrop and designated the ZSR-62. It was reportedly canceled in early 1990, but it has been described as an "active cancellation" system, capable of defeating some radars by mimicking the radar signal reflected from the B-2, and transmitting it one half wavelength out of phase with the real reflection. No further reliable information about the ZSR-62 or its importance to the B-2 has been published.

In combat, the B-2's information management system and cockpit displays should be able to "fuse" data from many sources. Radar imagery, for example, will be superimposed on maps of the target area, acquired by satellite and stored on the B-2. (One of the contractors in the B-2 program is Miltope, which specializes in high-density digital and optical disk drives for military applications.) The physical and electronic characteristics of known threats can also be stored and fused. If an SA-5 radar is detected, the system can display its location, its predicted area of coverage, and the bomber's projected track on the CRT; the crew can determine instantly whether a course change is necessary.

Much of the avionics system is based on thirteen common avionics control unit (ACU) processors built by Unisys, which carry out several functions that, in earlier systems, were performed by special-purpose computers: TF/TA, navigation, defensive systems, and stores management are all carried out by ACUs. Designed to meet stringent requirements for radiation-hardening and vibration tolerance (some of them are installed in the aft centerbody, between the engine exhausts), the ACUs can be expanded to handle more complex processing tasks through new software.

The navigation and radar systems have been tested on a modified Boeing C-135 transport, known as the flight test avionics laboratory (FTAL), which made its first flight in January 1987 and had flown more than 1,600 hours by early 1991. The FTAL was needed, because many radar modes cannot be adequately tested on a static test rig and some (such as SAR) cannot be demonstrated at all,

except in the air. In 1991, it was being prepared for a new series of flights to help prove the TF/TA modes on the B-2.

B-2 Weapons

The B-2 was designed from the ground up to cover all USAF bomber missions, conventional as well as nuclear. It was designed to carry a wide range of weapons; all the equipment needed to carry conventional weapons is included in the basic program cost, and a conventional weapons storage facility is being constructed at the first B-2 base, Whiteman Air Force Base.

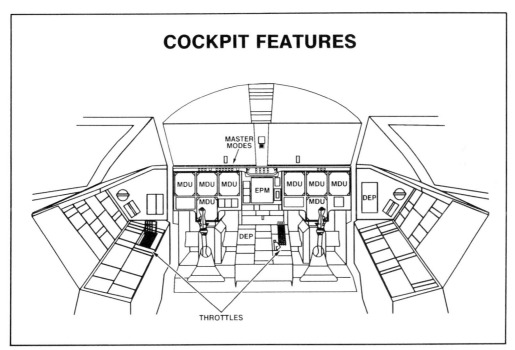

COCKPIT FEATURES

The B-2's roomy "glass cockpit" has full controls for both pilots. It has central control sticks, because the fly-by-wire flight control system does not require two-hand inputs. Both pilots have left-hand throttles and a right-hand data entry panel to program onboard computers. There are four six-inch-square, full-color multipurpose display unit screens on each side, and a central engine performance monitor screen. The "master mode" switches automatically configure the displays for takeoff and landing, cruise, and combat. Northrop

B-2 conventional loads can include up to eighty Mk82 500-pound bombs or thirty-six CBU-87/B cluster bombs. It will also be able to deliver some precision-guided munitions (PGMs). These will not necessarily be the types associated with current tactical aircraft, such as electro-optically-guided bombs (EOGBs) or laser-guided bombs (LGBs); the B-2 does not have a laser designator or, apparently, a datalink for EOGBs.

This does not mean that the B-2's PGM capability has been ignored, as some reports have suggested. Today's LGBs and EOGBs are refined versions of Vietnam-era weapons. They were effective in the Persian Gulf war, but have two fundamental limitations: the carrier aircraft has to guide them all or almost all the way to impact, either by lasing the target or by remote control, and their performance is reduced by clouds, fog, or smoke.

In the nineties, these weapons will be supplemented and eventually replaced by new "autonomous" PGMs that do not have to be guided to impact by the carrier aircraft. Instead, they will com-

The B-2 simulator faithfully reproduces the layout, look and feel of the real cockpit. CAE-Link

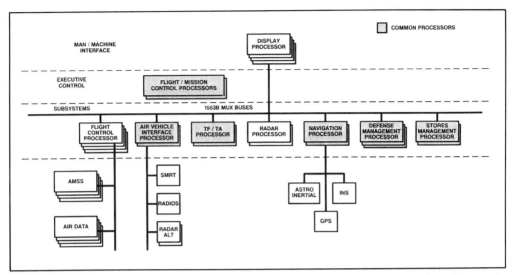

The "architecture" of the B-2's avionics system shows how all of its functions are overseen by the flight- and mission-control processors. Before the mission, these processors are programmed with complete mission plans, prepared on the ground and loaded into the system using memory cartridges. Many mission tasks can, therefore, be performed automatically; the crew's tasks are to monitor the system while concentrating on targets and threats. Northrop

pare sensed images of the target with images pre-programmed in their computer memory. Demonstration programs using IR and millimeter-wave (MMW) radar sensors were already under way in 1991.

This technology has been fused with another: the inertially aided munition (IAM), fitted with a simple inertial navigation system and steerable fins. Before release, the aircraft's bomb-aiming system programs the IAM's memory with the trajectory it has predicted for the weapon. If the IAM deviates from this trajectory (due to unpredicted wind or other minor errors), the guidance system will put it back on track. The IAM is not as accurate as a PGM, but it is far more accurate than a dumb bomb—particularly if it is released from a very accurate platform, such as a heavy bomber—and the guidance system is much cheaper than a PGM.

The combination of IAM guidance with the new, autonomous target seekers forms the basis of a new USAF/Navy weapon family called JDAM (Joint Direct Attack Munition). This program was launched in early 1992, and the weapons could enter service in the mid- to late nineties because much of the development work has already been carried out. The seekers and inertial guidance are synergistic: because the inertial guidance system will steer the bomb close to its target, the autonomous seeker has a smaller area to search and is easier to design and to program.

JDAM guidance kits can also be combined with "dispense-to-kill" weapons, such as the Sensor Fuzed Weapon (SFW), a 1,000-pound class bomb that ejects forty submunitions that will automatically attack any tank within a preprogrammed area.

As with today's PGMs, these new guidance systems will probably take the form of nose and tail kits attached to a family of standard bomb cases, including general purpose blast-fragmentation bombs, hard-target penetrators, and runway-destroying munitions.

The B-2's single most effective nonnuclear weapon, however, will probably be the Northrop AGM-137A Tri-Service Standoff Attack Missile (TSSAM). Revealed in June 1991 after five years as an undisclosed Special Access program (under the code name "Senior Pennant"),

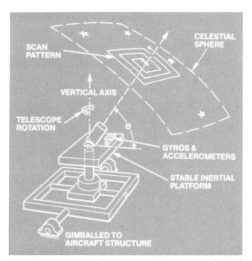

The astro-inertial navigation system is based on an electro-optical telescope mounted on a stabilized platform. The telescope scans the sky in a square pattern until it locates the first of several pre-programmed stars. It then continues to track and verify up to three stars per minute. The astro-inertial system is invulnerable to jamming or interference, requires no field calibration or on-ground alignment time, and is accurate to less than 1,000 feet, irrespective of flight time. Northrop

TSSAM traces its origin to the DARPA Pave Mover program of the late seventies. Pave Mover demonstrated the use of an airborne long-range radar to detect relocatable and mobile targets and submunition or unitary warheads to attack them.

In the early eighties, as plans were made to adapt Pave Mover technology for production systems, differences emerged in service requirements. The solution was to develop two new weapons: the low-cost, ballistic ATACMS for the Army and a more expensive, longer-range Stealth cruise missile for deep attack, whether launched from the ground or the air. This was at first known as Joint TACMS and later, as the program became more classified, as Senior Pennant. The 2,300-pound missile has a range of more than 100nm and is almost certainly jet-powered.

TSSAM's guidance system is autonomous. It is probably based on an inertial mid-course navigation system, combined with a terminal seeker that can image the target area, compare it to an image loaded into memory before launch, and guide the missile to a precise impact point. Autonomous systems may not be quite as precise as the best man-in-the-loop systems, but they should be capable of striking a bridge, a ship, a runway junction, or a specific building.

The exact nature of the TSSAM seeker is classified, but it could be an MMW radar, a compact SAR, or an imaging IR sensor. Lower-cost SAR and IIR autonomous guidance systems are being developed for glide bombs, so it would not be surprising to find such technology in the more exotic TSSAM. The fact that the weapon is designed to operate against moving targets such as ships and armoured formations suggests that a radar seeker is more likely to be fitted, because radar is inherently better at searching an area. A ship, for example, could cover 10km during the flight time of a TSSAM launched at maximum range. Radar is also less affected by low cloud and obscurants.

The B-2's main nuclear weapon is the B83 bomb. The B83 is described by the USAF as a "gravity weapon" because it is unguided and unpowered. It is the newest type of strategic nuclear bomb developed for the USAF, and was designed by the Department of Energy's Lawrence Livermore Nuclear Laboratory in California. It has a selectable yield between one and two megatons, and is the first production bomb to be designed for "laydown" delivery against hard, irregular targets. In such a delivery, the bomb is delay-fuzed so that the bomber can escape to a safe distance before the explosion. In contrast to airburst or contact fuzing, however, this means that the bomb must survive the initial impact with the ground and land without bouncing or rolling.

The B-2 was also designed to use the Boeing AGM-131A SRAM II missile. The SRAM (Short-Range Attack Missile) II was a direct replacement for the original Boeing AGM-69 SRAM, which was designed in the sixties. It consisted of a 200-kiloton warhead, a rocket motor, and a Litton laser-gyro inertial naviga-

tion system. The SRAM II was due to enter service in 1993, but its development was terminated as part of the nuclear weapons cutbacks ordered by President Bush in September 1991.

The B-2's early title—the Advanced Technology Bomber—would be appropriate even if the B-2 was not designed to be stealthy. Its unconventional design makes it more efficient than a normal aircraft. With its FBW flight control system, the B-2 is efficient at both high and low altitudes, without the mechanical complexity and aerodynamic compromises inherent in a swing-wing shape. The accuracy of its navigation system and the acuity and range of its primary sensor are unsurpassed by any aircraft.

Combining all these features with the discipline of low observables, and launching the program when virtually the only Stealth aircraft in the air were a few F-117A prototypes, was nobody's recipe for a trouble-free program. Certainly, nobody expected that it would be cheap. By the time AV-1 was rolled out, controversy about the bomber's price and effectiveness was mounting. The political consensus that had supported it throughout the eighties was wavering, in the face of seismic shifts in global politics. The project emerged from the black into a storm of controversy.

Chapter 3

Changing Times, Changing Missions

Like a submarine, the B-2 is a small target in a large ocean.

—B-2 designer Irving Waaland

The B-2 was designed in 1981, primarily for nuclear warfare against the Soviet Union. No pundit—left, right, or center—predicted then that the communist world would be turned upside down in a decade, in history's biggest revolution.

As the world has changed, the USAF has rested its case for the B-2 increasingly on other, non-nuclear missions. Opponents charge the Pentagon with weaseling and back-pedaling. Flexibility may be a better word—when developing a major weapon takes fifteen years and the world's political structure can turn turtle in fifteen months, and, as we saw in August 1991, threaten to flip over again in a matter of hours.

It is probably fair to say, in the early fall of 1991, that the B-2 is considered to be a weapon of conventional deterrence with a secondary nuclear mission, rather than the other way around. Conventional deterrence is vital.

Lessons of Desert Storm

The single largest of all the "lessons" of the Persian Gulf war has usually been overlooked. Saddam Hussein rolled over Kuwait because it suited Iraq's needs (when you are deep in debt, it is always attractive to rob your bank)

and because he was convinced that nobody would throw him out again. His neighbors could not do so and, in his view, the likely costs would dissuade anyone else from trying. The lesson is that, in August 1990, conventional deterrence failed.

Desert Storm has been cited as an example of a new world order in which the United States, as the only superpower, need no longer fear Soviet action when it intervenes on an ally's behalf. But the end of the superpower balance may be a mixed blessing. Many leaders no longer feel that they have to place a call to Moscow before they invade, and that factor may be destabilizing.

The US military is changing to reflect the reduced threat of nuclear war, the dimming likelihood of a major conventional war in Europe, and the recognition that US national interests are now increasingly tied to the ability of US conventional forces to underpin the strength of its allies throughout the world. As part of these changes, the USAF is on the verge of the biggest changes in its structure in forty years.

Strategic Air Command is to be eliminated, along with Tactical Air Command and Military Airlift Command.

Bombers, fighters, and strike and support aircraft will be assigned to another new organization, Air Combat Command. A much reduced ICBM force is being transferred to the control of a new Strategic Command, which will also control the Navy's strategic missiles. Airlifters and many tankers will be assigned to a new organization, Air Mobility Command.

Air Combat Command is intended to bring the USAF's "shooters" and their support assets together so that, during peacetime, they train in the kind of organization that had to be constructed for the Desert Shield and Desert Storm operations. Within the new command, the B-2's role will be increasingly domi-

nated by conventional missions, as will that of the B-1s and remaining B-52s. It appears that only a few B-52Hs, armed with the AGM-129 Advanced Cruise Missile, will retain a primarily nuclear role.

President Bush's weapon cuts of September 1991 further emphasized the B-2's conventional mission. With the cancellation of SRAM II, the B-2 has only gravity weapons to attack nuclear targets. At the same time, the decision to end SAC's thirty-year-long alert will release more of its bombers and crews to train for conventional missions in concert with other forces.

The change in the B-2's mission demonstrated the overwhelming differ-

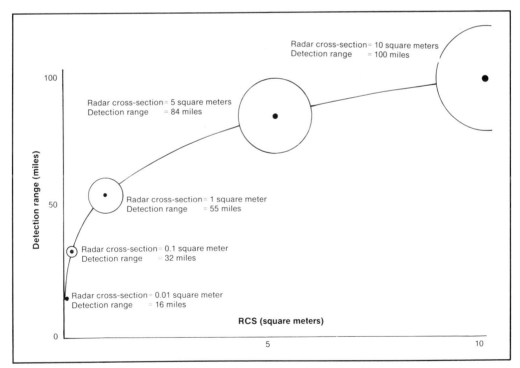

The range at which a radar will detect a target does not vary directly with the target's RCS, but with its fourth root. Therefore, RCS *must be reduced by a factor of 100 or more to achieve major reductions in detection range.* Bill Sweetman

ence between the bomber and cther strategic nuclear delivery systems; ICBMs, SLBMs, and nuclear cruise missiles are entirely useless for non-nuclear missions, but a bomber fleet can be converted from one role to the other within hours.

Most bomber types developed for nuclear attack have, at one time or another, been used to deliver conventional bombs or adapted for other roles.

The difference between the B-2 and most other nuclear-age bombers is that conventional missions have been considered from the start of the program.

The B-2's conventional capability springs from its warload and range, its survivability, and its avionics suite. Its warload and unrefueled mission radius are similar to the B-52's, and several times larger than the figures for any smaller aircraft.

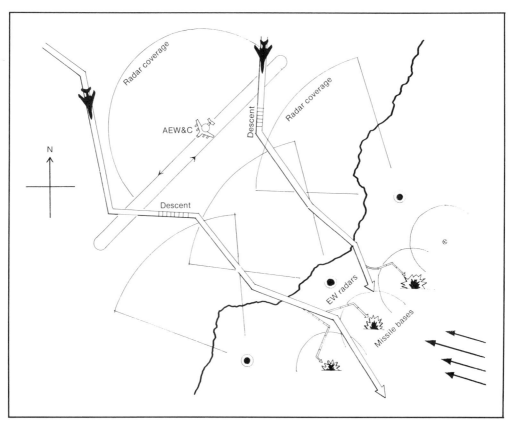

Contemporary bomber tactics: bombers approaching from the northwest cannot avoid detection by airborne early warning and control (AEW&C) aircraft or an overlapping chain of ground-based electronic warfare radars. By changing course and dropping to low altitude, they can delay detection. The chain of missile sites will, nevertheless, be prewarned. While they can be attacked with SRAM missiles, the fighters approaching from the southeast cannot be so readily countered, and some of the bombers will be lost.

Range opens up many options. Short-range aircraft have to be moved within range of their targets, either by using an aircraft carrier or by establishing a forward base, both of which take time and are difficult to do covertly. With one refueling, the B-2 can cover virtually all the world's land-mass from the continental United States, Guam, or Diego Garcia.

Survivability makes the ability to carry large loads over long distances much more useful than it was in the case of the B-52. Because of its Stealth characteristics, the B-2 can fly against defended targets without the aid of shorter-range escort, jamming, or defense suppression aircraft.

Finally, the B-2's navigation and weapon-delivery systems provide capabilities that would be difficult if not impossible to duplicate in a smaller aircraft. Features such as a fully redundant navigation system; dual-channel, high-resolution radar; and very large antennas have a direct bearing on the system's performance and the probability of being able to complete a mission despite equipment failures or poor weather. Even if it were technically possible to fit such devices on a smaller aircraft, it is economically undesirable to put so much expensive electronic systems on an aircraft with a mere 6,000-pound warload.

Know-nothing commentators and politicians frequently attempt to hoot down claims about the B-2's conventional capability with such statements as, "Nobody would risk an $800 million bomber to destroy a $500,000 bridge."

The basic fallacy behind this sort of statement is the implication that the military value of a target is proportional to its cash value. If the $500,000 bridge is carrying hostile forces on their way to attack friendly troops, it could obviously be worth expending more than $500,000-worth of munitions to destroy it. To take an historical example: it was hardly worth sending twelve P-38 Lightnings on a 1,000-mile round-trip on the chance of shooting down one Mitsubishi G4M bomber, unless Admiral Yamamoto was riding in it.

It is also strange, to say the least, to think that a commander would plan a mission on the basis of the price of the equipment placed at risk. The commander's duty is to accomplish his mission with the minimum risk to the people under his command; material losses are secondary. In strictly military terms, in fact, the B-2 is the ideal weapon for many missions.

In mid-1991, the USAF analyzed a number of Desert Storm missions flown by F-117s or conventional aircraft. A typical, conventional package included sixteen strike aircraft, carrying precision-guided munitions (PGMs); sixteen fighter escorts; four escort jammers; eight defense-suppression strike aircraft and Wild Weasels; and seven KC-135 tankers to support the fleet. The total of forty-nine aircraft had well over ninety crew members on board.

An F-117 mission needed only eight strike aircraft to achieve the same damage, because the F-117's Stealth permitted a more accurate attack profile. The F-117s were supported by two KC-135s: ten aircraft and eighteen-plus crew. Two B-2s could have flown the same mission from Diego Garcia without tanker support, with a total crew of four.

For other Desert Storm missions, the B-2 would have reduced sorties still further and would have given the commanders more time to launch attacks. F-117 attacks on nuclear sites, bunkers, and aircraft shelters north of Baghdad could not be carried out until air superiority had been achieved over most of

Iraq, allowing tankers and their escorts to fly north of Saudi Arabia. B-2s could have hit those targets from Day 1, using PGMs.

Military-industrial complexes north of Baghdad were ideal targets for B-52s, but F-117s had to go in first to suppress the defenses. The F-117s were needed for higher-priority targets, so these raids were not carried out until late in the forty-three-day war. Again, B-2s could have struck the same targets unescorted.

Some aspects of the Persian Gulf war, moreover, were extremely favorable to conventional tactical air power. The coalition forces had several months to bed-down their aircraft in large, modern bases designed to US standards. The bases were located in a country immediately adjacent to the aggressor nation, but were safe from attack.

None of these conditions will necessarily apply in future conflicts. There may be less preparation time. Local bases may be small, restricting the

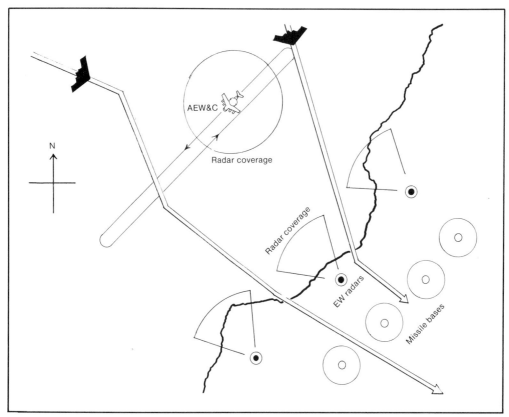

B-2 tactics: a sharp cut in radar detection range makes the AEW&C aircraft much easier to evade, and opens up gaps in the coverage of ground-based radars, even at high level. With no early warning, and with targets at their maximum effective range, surface-to-air missiles are unable to engage the bombers effectively.

number of aircraft in-country. Fuel supplies may not be infinite. Bases and fuel supplies may be subject to attack by insurgents or infiltrators armed with mortars, rockets, or shoulder-fired SAMs.

With no warning time, the B-2's ability to launch a first sortie from the United States, with follow-up sorties generated from the United States, Guam, or Diego Garcia, could be critical. Had Saddam Hussein driven directly into Saudi Arabia after invading Kuwait, the USAF notes, a force of sixty B-2s could have delivered 1,200 tons of ordnance on the first day and 600 tons the next day. It would have been twenty-two days before enough tactical fighters and tankers could have been deployed to deliver the same load.

Armed with AGM-137 TSSAMs or JDAMs, the B-2 is a unique conventional weapon that can damage militarily important targets with very little warning. The B-2 can hit such targets as bridges, road junctions, ammunition dumps, and fuel farms with enough ordnance to close them or substantially reduce their capacity, blunting an offensive within hours of the decision to fight. A single B-2 could deliver enough weapons against an airfield to both crater its runways and damage other facilities, such as its fuel supplies.

The B-2's ability to strike from US bases reduces or eliminates the need to secure the approval of third parties before taking military action, and preserves strategic surprise as long as possible. The bomber's survivability and the advantage of surprise give the mission a good chance of success, while sophisticated avionics and sensors ensure, as far as possible, that weapons will not go where they are not aimed, so that civilian casualties can be minimized.

TSSAM is a particularly good match for the B-2, which will be able to carry as many TSSAMs as eight tactical aircraft and deliver them without the aid of an offboard targeting system, such as Joint STARS. Using its high-resolution APQ-181 radar, a single, unescorted B-2 will be able to detect and map targets, and initialize and launch up to sixteen TSSAMs, while remaining well outside the range at which any defensive system will be able to detect the low observable bomber.

The B-2 Versus Mobile Targets

The TSSAM and B-2 combination poses an enormous threat to surface ships. In most cases, the B-2 will be able to identify individual ships in a group without being detected itself, select the most important targets, and attack them—and do all these things from well outside the range of the surface combatants' own defensive missiles. The stealthy missiles, following a low-altitude attack profile, will be undetectable until they are very close to their targets.

USAF officers are wary of talking about the B-2's effectiveness against ships (they remember what happened to Billy Mitchell), but its combination of range, ability to search an area, and lethal long-range weaponry may make it a greater threat to the ship than the submarine has been.

Ships are not the only mobile target against which the B-2 could be used. Another lesson of the Persian Gulf war is that ballistic missiles represent a threat to regional stability, which is all out of proportion to their military effectiveness. The extraordinary efforts the coalition forces devoted to "the great Scud chase" around Iraq were necessary because successful Scud attacks on Israel could have forced Israeli retaliation and splintered the coalition. Future missiles will be more accurate, more lethal, and more mobile.

In future conflicts, the B-2 could be a particularly useful weapon against ballistic missiles. With foreseeable or available technology, the bomber is the only long-range system that can find a target at an undetermined position within a defined area, identify it, complete an attack on it while its position is still known, and confirm its destruction. All four of these steps are critical to holding a relocatable target at risk, and none can be accomplished reliably with any other combination of systems.

The B-2's capability against mobile targets is particularly important, because it can penetrate and survive without using terrain cover, which allows the bomber's sensors to scan a much larger area than they could if they were mounted on a low-flying B-1. Flying at 50,000 feet, a B-2 should be able to see a target the size of a Scud launcher at a distance of 100 miles or more. The ability to survive at medium altitude enables the B-2's already considerable range to be translated into endurance, increasing the area that the bomber can search on a given mission.

The foregoing discussion is based on the use of smart weapons such as JDAM or TSSAM. One thing is certain about such weapons, however: they will always be more expensive than dumb bombs. They will never replace the simple high-explosive bomb and will probably never be a majority of the weapons in the inventory of any service.

In fact, some commentators since the war have argued that the massive B-52 strikes against Iraqi troops did as much to shorten the ground war as the better publicized use of precision weapons. Direct damage was backed up by indirect effects, including the shattered morale among troops subjected to the thundering hell of a B-52 attack, and the Iraqis response to the attacks, digging in their tanks until they were little use

The importance of Stealth in future operations is underlined by the increasing use of AEW&C aircraft, which threaten the low-altitude sanctuary in which most strike aircraft now operate. One Ilyushin Il-76 Main-stay, of the type seen here, was exported to Iraq before the Persian Gulf War; another Il-76 transport was locally adapted to an AEW&C aircraft. Department of Defense

except as pillboxes and sitting targets for precision weapons.

The comparison that the USAF is not allowed to make on the record is between the B-52s and the US Navy's prize possessions, its aircraft carriers. About thirty B-52s delivered 25 per cent of the munitions dropped on Iraq by US air forces: almost half the total delivered by land-based tactical aircraft, and actually more than was delivered by the Navy and Marine Corps combined. The reason was range. The carriers were forced to stand off in deeper, safer waters—a billion-dollar Navy combatant, the Aegis cruiser *Princeton,* came closer than anyone wanted to being sunk by a mine in the Gulf—and their aircraft could not sustain high sortie rates, even with the help of Air Force tankers.

The B-2's Nuclear Mission

The B-2 still has a nuclear mission. The risk and fear of such a war have receded, but any rational defense plan must acknowledge that a resurgent nuclear threat could emerge in far less time than it would take to reconstruct a deterrent force, as long as large numbers of nuclear weapons exist.

The United States maintains three different classes of weapon which threaten, or, as the USAF says, "hold at risk" hostile targets: bombers, ICBMs, and submarine-launched ballistic missiles.

The bomber has unique features that make it an important component of a deterrent force. The bomber's large warload and its ability to attack multiple targets on a single mission allow it to hold more targets at risk than a missile. This attribute of the bomber was highlighted by the new Strategic Arms Reduction Treaty, which treated one bomber, with 16 to 24 megaton-class warheads, as the equivalent of one missile with ten smaller MIRVs.

The bomber is also an economical user of weapons. Many important targets must be allocated two or more weapons to ensure their destruction because of the inevitable technical failures. If they are missile warheads, both must

One way of installing a large radar on a small platform, and making airborne early warning more affordable, is to use a physically fixed, electronically steered "active array."

This Fairchild Metro will be used by the Royal Swedish Air Force to test the Ericsson PS-90 radar, which may form the basis of a "mini-AWACS" in the nineties. Fairchild

be fired. If the second warhead is carried by a bomber, the crew can image the target on radar, determine whether the first weapon has hit it, and conserve their weapon if the target has been destroyed.

The bomber can be re-used after the first round of strikes. Although first strikes would be launched from bomber bases, the USAF has made a point of observing that the B-2 could use any one of hundreds of runways in the United States.

As well as being able to threaten many targets even in a protracted war, the B-2 is particularly effective against some targets that are resistant to missile attack. These include targets that may be in any one of a number of locations, such as military units, and relocatable missiles.

Military and command objectives will also be on the target list. The Soviet Union exploited the fact that, while a missile silo must be close to the surface of the ground in order to fire, a command bunker may be buried hundreds of feet below the surface. If the ground is hard, the target may be safe from all but the largest surface- or air-bursting warheads. However, the logic of treaty limits on the number of delivery vehicles caused large unitary ICBM warheads to be replaced by smaller 200 to 500 kiloton MIRVs.

Another attribute of the penetrating bomber which is not always appreciated is that it is economically competitive with other survivable, mobile means of delivering nuclear weapons. Exact comparisons are virtually impossible to make—comparing the life-cycle cost of a submarine to that of a bomber is not exactly easy—but the fundamental difference is that the bomber both transports and delivers the weapon. Most other systems, such as the SLBM, use both a large, sophisticated, and expensive missile, with its own high-precision guidance system, and a specially developed vehicle, such as a submarine, to transport the missiles.

Numbers prepared in 1989 by the Union of Concerned Scientists (an anti-nuclear lobby) showed that the B-2 was competitive with land-based mobile missiles on a cost-per-warhead basis. Comparisons show that the only system that is decisively cheaper than the bomber is the silo-launched missile, but as we have seen, it is not an adequate deterrent.

Another B-2 alternative that has been proposed from time to time is a non-stealthy aircraft carrying cruise missiles. There are two main problems with such a concept. The first is cost: cruise missiles are more costly to build and maintain than bombs. A cruise-missile carrier aircraft derived from a transport (the venerable Boeing 707 would be a perfectly adequate choice) would be cheaper than the B-2, but not by as much as one might think given the weapon-integration task. The second objection is that a cruise-based system can be defeated by moving the defensive perimeter outwards (using bigger fighters and more tankers), so that the carrier aircraft can be engaged before they are within missile range of their targets.

All of the B-2's offensive capability, however, is realistic only if it can be used. History is replete with examples of expensive weapons that were so valuable that they were never put to proper use, such as battleships in World War I. Here lies the other fallacy behind the B-2-versus-bridge argument. The commander's decision to use one or another weapon rests not so much on their price tags, but on the chance that they will accomplish their missions and survive.

The B-2 Versus Air-Defense Systems

Survivability is always critical to military aircraft, but more so to the B-2 than most. One reason is that a B-2 is a large and scarce military asset, and combat losses would have an important political impact on the management of any conflict. (This was the case when B-52 loss rates peaked during the Line-backer II raids on North Vietnam.)

Also, if tactical aircraft are threatened by improvements in the defenses, it is always possible to assign more resources to jamming and defense suppression, as was done in Vietnam. The unique military utility of the B-2, however, depends to a great extent on its long range and its freedom from support; its own inherent survivability is much more important.

The B-2's survivability, whether in strategic or tactical missions, depends to a large degree on Stealth. What made its design particularly challenging was that it was intended to defeat the most intri-cate, best-equipped air-defense system ever deployed: the strategic defenses of the Soviet Union.

Whatever may happen to the former Soviet Union, its air-defense system was not unique or a factor of its politics. It is the kind of system that is needed or desired by any country that feels the threat of air attack and, increasingly, large regional powers will put together systems like it for their own defenses.

The Soviet system is based on a layered, interconnected structure. It is designed to start destroying bombers as far from their targets as possible, and to continue to whittle down the force until the shortest-range elements of the system can concentrate on only a few targets.

The first line of defense extends up to 1,000 miles from the outermost usable bases, well above the Arctic Circle. Its eyes are over-the-horizon (OTH) radars, which have long range but relatively poor ability to track individual targets; forward-located, surface-based radars;

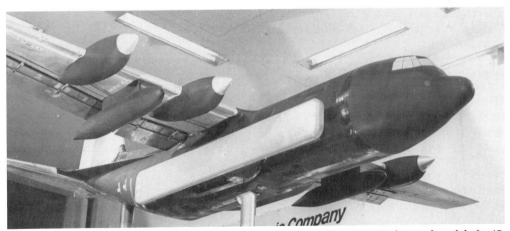

If active-array technology permits the installation of an AWACS-sized antenna on an aircraft the size of the Metro, it can clearly be used to put a much larger radar on a bigger platform. This is a wind tunnel model of a 45-foot-long antenna developed by Lockheed, mounted on the side of a C-130. Lockheed

and, increasingly, airborne radar systems, such as the Ilyushin Mainstay, which, like the equivalent AWACS, can track low-flying targets against ground clutter.

The teeth of the outer defense line are very large, long-range fighters with no direct equivalent in the West, such as the Mikoyan MiG-31 Foxhound. The formidable MiG-31 has a heavy armament, impressive range, and a massive electronically scanned radar, and is a lookdown, shoot-down (LDSD) system that can engage low-flying targets. Not only does the MiG-31 engage targets itself, but it also transmits target information back to the air-defense control center.

The next element of the layered defense consists of shorter-range, one-pilot fighters. Because of their range, these fighters defend a smaller zone of airspace around their base, and operate within the range of ground-based radar. The majority of the 2,200-plus fighters assigned to air defense of the Soviet Union fall into this category, and air-defense zones cover the entire country. These zone-defense fighters operate with the aid of a "ground environment," including radar, computers, and control systems.

The number of surface-to-air missiles deployed to defend the continental United States is zero. The Soviet Union has several thousand sites and has deployed formidable systems, such as the Almaz S-300PMU—known to the West, before glasnost, as the SA-10 Grumble. The S-300PMU is rather like a scaled-up version of the US Patriot, capable of multiple simultaneous engagements down to near ground level.

The USAF argues that the B-2 will defeat air-defense systems because it cannot be "consistently detected, tracked, or engaged at militarily useful ranges in typical operational scenarios."

It is important to remember that the bomber is not dead even if it is detected. Air defense combines three inter-related functions—surveillance, fire control, and kill—each of which must be carried out with 80 per cent probability of success in order to achieve an overall kill probability of 50 per cent.

Moreover, air defenses must be able to survive direct attacks, resist countermeasures, and work despite the variation of the environment, including severe weather and fluctuations in natural radiation sources.

The ability to detect the target against natural clutter, according to the USAF, "is often the limiting factor, particularly in the case of proposed unconventional air defense schemes."

Stealth does not imply invisibility. The effect of Stealth is to reduce the range at which a radar or any other sensor can detect the B-2. Chains of ground-based radars, located so that their areas of coverage against conventional targets overlap one another, are too far apart to cover the entire perimeter against the B-2. If a radar does detect a B-2, the bomber will be out of range very quickly as its crew takes evasive action, and its projected position will be uncertain. The fighter sent to catch the B-2 is hampered by reduced effectiveness of its onboard radar and IRST.

B-2 tactics are based on the fact that Stealth reduces the bomber's detectability without affecting the ability of its electronic surveillance systems to detect radar emissions. If a radar is detected, the onboard systems will identify it, locate its position and compute its volume of coverage, which can be superimposed on the B-2's computer map display. The crew can then detour around or beneath the detection zone, with the aid of computer programs which can indicate the best use of terrain to mask their aircraft from the radar.

The foundation of modern bomber tactics is that the bomber flies alone. On the other hand, this does not rule out the coordination of bomber ingress routes, in space and time, in order to put the defenses to as much trouble as possible. The key is to keep the bombers close together in time but separated in space. Thus, the defending commander has little time to deal with the targets before they reach the next zone, and his controllers are overtaxed. At the same time, however, the bombers are crossing his perimeter hundreds of miles apart, so that his fighters are limited, by their speed and their range, in their ability to go from one engagement point to another.

The same philosophy can apply to countering SAMs, the difference being that the spatial separation between the bombers is best expressed in terms of the compass rather than the map. Few SAM systems can engage targets simultaneously in diametrically different directions without operating at much less than their peak efficiency.

The B-2's ability to evade radar has been controversial, often pitting expert against expert but more often leading to a thermonuclear exchange of misinformation. The USAF has never asserted that the bomber is invisible. "Some big, powerful radars," the USAF acknowledges in a document released in 1990, "do have a useful detection capability [against the B-2]. In response, the B-2 could employ evasive routing, flying low

This Westinghouse airship prototype, flown in 1991, illustrates a low-tech approach to airborne early warning. The envelope can accommodate a large antenna, allowing a relatively unsophisticated radar to detect low-flying targets effectively. Such technology is well within the reach of many nations. Westinghouse

to reduce coverage or using stand-off weapons to attack targets in the vicinity of those radars. Some of the larger capable radars could be mobile. But the B-2's crew could detect the radiation from these radars long before the radar detects the bomber (a simple matter of physics) and then avoid the threat."

As for airborne radars, the USAF claims: "Stealth technology essentially takes these threats out of the picture." Apparently, the B-2's design RCS is low enough that airborne radars, with less power and smaller antennas than ground-based radars, will not detect it at a tactically useful range.

The formidable S-300PMU surface-to-air missile system, known to Western intelligence (in pre-glasnost days) as the SA-10, was one of the threats making the design of the B-1's electronic jamming system almost impossible. Now, it is advertised for international sale and is likely to form part of an increasing number of defensive systems worldwide.

A number of conventional and unconventional detection systems have been touted as effective against the B-2. One of them is very-high-frequency (VHF) radar. VHF radar operates at lower frequencies and longer wavelengths than the microwave frequencies used by most radars; older radars used VHF, but it was generally superseded by microwave systems because they are more compact and much more accurate. However, the Soviet Union still used some VHF radars for strategic defense up to 1991.

According to the USAF, "the B-2's design can deal with [VHF] radar." It is

probably a safe guess that the deep-section Hexcel honeycomb RAM on the B-2's leading edge is designed for broadband effectiveness, extending down to VHF. In any case, the USAF adds, "VHF is not a particularly effective surveillance tool. VHF radars have serious problems in detecting low flyers and coping with man-made interference and jamming."

A USAF "red team" assigned to find ways of defeating the B-2 investigated more than fifty unconventional air-defense concepts, some of which were actually tested. For instance, acoustic detection schemes spurred the USAF to look at aircraft acoustic signatures, propagation, and interference phenomena. Acoustic arrays were integrated into an experimental detection system, and detection ranges against different targets at different speeds and altitudes were measured.

The USAF found that an acoustic sensor might have a range of five miles, but there are drawbacks. The sensitivity of the sensors was degraded by wind noise; coverage was unreliable, because atmospheric propagation was inconsistent; and snow, ice, and rain could stop the microphones from working properly.

Claims by Australian developers of the OTH Jindalee radar that OTH can detect the B-2 are seen in a different perspective by the USAF. OTH may be able to detect small targets, because its extremely long wavelengths (in the 10-meter realm) are unaffected by RAM, and most practical shapes are resonant to OTH. The problem is that OTH is not very accurate. It is used to provide early warning of a raid and to "cue" more accurate, shorter-range sensors, which can then search a given area for the target. These sensors (such as airborne radars) are negated by the B-2.

The USAF also investigated ultra-wideband (UWB) radar, otherwise known as impulse or carrier-free radar, which has been touted as an anti-Stealth measure. UWB radar differs fundamentally from conventional radar because it emits a "square" pulse of energy, rather than a sinusoidal wave. Because RAM works through a resonant mechanism based on the radar's waveform, it is ineffective against UWB radar.

The USAF's objections to UWB as an anti-Stealth measure are rooted in economics: UWB requires an enormous amount of development work before it can operate at the power levels required to detect aircraft at long range. "Basically," says a USAF officer, "we concluded that the same results could be achieved more cheaply by proliferating conventional radars." That technique, however, would not defeat the B-2 at an affordable cost.

B-2 opponents have touted a whole range of potential anti-Stealth detection systems that would defeat the B-2 by technical means. So far, any detailed scrutiny has shown that their claims have been overblown and that no affordable means exists to negate Stealth and prevent the B-2 and other Stealth aircraft from performing their missions with a reasonable chance of success. Instead, B-2 opponents have turned to another weapon: politics and the budget.

Chapter 4

A Billion Here, a Billion There

Didn't we invent the airplanes and then think after we had invented them that that was all you was supposed to do with them? European nations . . . know what altitude of the elements the next war will be fought in.

—Will Rogers

In 1986, the USAF announced that the first operational B-2 wing would be located at Whiteman Air Force Base (AFB), near Kansas City, Missouri. It was a surprise decision, because Whiteman had not hosted large aircraft since the sixties, when a B-47 wing gave way to Minuteman missiles. Whiteman met some important qualifications, though. It was far from either coast, providing the longest possible warning time against the worst-case attack, a low-trajectory shot from a submarine-launched ballistic missile. It was closer to target areas than some candidate bases (those in Texas or Oklahoma, for instance). It also had plenty of space for new construction, which could be done without disrupting other operations.

Although the USAF has not announced a planned initial operating capability (IOC) date for the B-2, Col. John J. Politi, commander of the USAF's 100th Air Division, has said that "the bulk of our B-2 people will arrive in 1994." The critical factor, however, will be the availability of enough aircraft to form a full squadron.

The first—and on current plans the only—B-2 unit will be the 509th Bombardment Wing, with two eight-aircraft squadrons. It flew FB-111As from Pease AFB, New Hampshire, until last autumn, when it was inactivated and its aircraft were transferred to Tactical Air Command. The 509th is directly descended from the 509th Composite Wing, which was formed in 1944 to deliver the first US atomic weapons.

New buildings at Whiteman are scheduled to include sixteen maintenance docks, ten "canopy" shelters in the alert area, and four other enclosed buildings, providing covered storage for all of its B-2s. Today, Strategic Air Command (SAC) bombers are parked in the open, except while undergoing major maintenance. There is no reason that B-2s cannot be stored outdoors, according to Northrop, but the USAF has elected to build shelters to protect its long-term investment in the aircraft (as one Northrop executive puts it, "you don't buy a Lamborghini and park it on the street") and ease maintenance in bad weather. The shelters will also be equipped with deluge fire-suppression systems, which could recover most of the investment in the buildings if they save one aircraft.

The original plan called for the first B-2s to reach Whiteman by September 1991. The reasons that this did not happen and (at the time of writing) may not happen at all are complex and only partly connected with the technology or management of the program or with the aircraft's performance.

The first flight of the B-2 was originally scheduled for November 1987. That date went by the board due to the 1983 wing redesign, which cost the program a year. Then, cumulative glitches and problems, not one of them major in itself, delayed completion of the first B-2, AV-1.

AV-1 is not a prototype, in the normal sense. Traditionally, an aircraft development, the first aircraft and the production tooling are designed and built in parallel. The first aircraft is built on adjustable fixtures called "soft tools"; as design changes are made, the tools are adjusted and as the design is finalized, the soft tools are replaced, one by one, with fixed, heavy-duty hard tools that will retain their dimensions and exact tolerances throughout the production run. The prototype aircraft may be identical to the production aircraft from a distance, but it may be heavier, production parts may not be interchangeable, and even the dimensions may be measurably different. This matters little if the first prototype's task is to evaluate basic flying qualities and aerodynamic performance; the air is tolerant of such minor variations.

The snags with the B-2 design were that it was virtually impossible to produce using existing technology, and that it would be prohibitively expensive to build if it could be built at all. This was because Northrop's concept for RCS control was unforgiving. The external shape of every aircraft had to conform exactly to the low-RCS shape defined by the supercomputers, and everything had to fit perfectly. Electromagnetic laws, it seemed, were even less tolerant of deviation than aerodynamics.

A conventional prototype, therefore, would not be able to demonstrate the bomber's crucial Stealth characteristics. Even if the hand-built prototype was stealthy, it would not necessarily mean that the slightly different production configuration would be stealthy. The answer was to build all 132 aircraft on hard production tooling, but this meant a revolution in aircraft design and manufacture.

The shape of a conventional aircraft is basically defined in terms of "stations," which are cross-sectional views of the aircraft taken at different points from nose to tail or from wingtip to wingtip. After the aircraft is designed on paper in this way, the production engineers will use these stations to define three-dimensional parts, interpreting the drawings to fill in the shape between stations. This is acceptable for aerodynamic purposes, but apparently not for Stealth.

Northrop's solution was to extend changes they had started in the early seventies. The development of computers, graphic displays, and other tools had reached a point by the end of the decade where many engineers worked at a computer screen rather than a drawing board. A computer-aided design (CAD) system allows the designer to modify the drawing on the screen, change its scale, visualize it from different points, and rotate it.

On the assembly line, more and more tasks were being done by automated machines guided by computers. Machining, riveting, and building up laminates from layers of graphite fiber tape were being done or could be done under electronic control, with great consistency and the potential for built-in inspection.

With a new, very long, valuable program ahead of it, Northrop had the opportunity to adopt a completely new way of doing business. As the company renovated its massive plant at Pico Rivera, where much of the B-2 was to be built, it followed a new concept: computer-integrated manufacturing (CIM).

At Pico Rivera, the image of CAD became the reality. The external shape of the new bomber was defined in a computer database, not in terms of sections and stations, but in its totality; the database could define the precise three-dimensional coordinates of any point on the skin. The database was housed on banks of tape drives and managed by a Cray supercomputer.

Connected to the database were more than 400 computer work stations at Pico Rivera; the database was shared with major subcontractors Boeing and LTV and their own engineers. As detail design proceeded, the engineers could work from the outside in; as the design of each part was completed, it was added to the database. The computer system grew to define the shape and location of every component of the B-2, quite literally down to the smallest fastener.

Actually, this detail is not too hard to achieve once the system is in place. Since many small parts (fasteners and couplings, for example) are identical, the database needs to record their complete characteristics only once, storing only the location and orientation of the individual parts. The most challenging part of the computer integration process, "the most complex information we handled," was establishing the basic external shape of the aircraft.

The same database is used to control machine tools and industrial robots, to design tooling and forms, and to generate data for tooling alignment. An engineer developing an operating program for a machine tool, for example, can do so on a CAD work station, draw-

ing on the actual characteristics of the component itself; the engineer no longer has to "re-interpret" another engineer's drawing. The same applies to automatic tape-laying and other composite manufacturing processes.

Quite early in the program, the database took over from the first "engineering fixture" produced to support the B-2 design, so that the aircraft became the first of such complexity to be created without a true mock-up. The mock-up, a full-size model of a new airplane, has long been a symbol of human imperfectibility in engineering—a cumbersome device, but necessary to prevent gross errors (such as one engineer's hydraulic tube running through another's fire-bottle) and to catch some of the smaller fit problems. The database not only replaces the mock-up in this respect, but does so better. The engineer can visualize interference problems on the screen as the component takes shape; before the design is released, it is run through a validation process that checks every point against the database. "First-part" fit errors have been reduced by a factor of six, compared with previous programs, eliminating a great deal of tedious and costly reworking of not-quite-right components.

The computer system has opened the way to a change that is as much cultural as it is technological. Most program managers now assert that manufacturing and logistics engineers are involved in the design process, ensuring, for example, that components are designed in a way that lends itself to automation and that components are readily accessible. Within the B-2 program, however, the manufacturing and logistics groups can review engineering progress in near-real time; because of this, they can be (and have been) given authority over design release. The engineers alone cannot release a component over the objections of manufacturing or logistics. Instead, the different groups cooperate on the design, and, through Northrop's CAD, can implement a producibility or supportability improvement two to five times faster than by using a conventional drafting method. Northrop people are now carrying this cultural change into the California educational system, pressing the aeronautical-engineering departments to put more stress on production technology.

In a very real sense, the database is the B-2, and the airplanes on the production line are a representation of it, along with the electronic instruction codes for the robots, illustrations for logistics manuals, and models for wind tunnel and RCS testing.

The decision to build every B-2 as a production aircraft made long-term sense. It allowed realistic Stealth testing early in the program and it meant that all the aircraft but one—AV-2, which is stuffed with gauges to measure loads on the structure—could be made operational. However, it also ruled out the kind of making-things-fit and impromptu modification work that would normally be carried out on a prototype aircraft. Building AV-1 as an operational aircraft would make it much easier to build subsequent aircraft, but it made AV-1 much more difficult.

Under some political pressure, the USAF announced in late October 1988— before election day—that the B-2 would be rolled out on November 22. The rollout went ahead as planned, but AV-1 went back into the shop, so that a considerable amount of work that needed to be done before the aircraft flew could be completed. AV-1 made its first flight on July 17, 1989, making a low-speed, gear-down hop from Palmdale to Edwards.

By that time, however, technical problems with the program had been overshadowed by political and financial snags. The B-2 manufacturing plan called for the production rate to rise as the aircraft came down the "learning curve." The learning curve is a basic manufacturing concept, which depicts how the number of hours required to build each successive aircraft decreases as snags in early aircraft are overcome and workers learn to do their jobs more efficiently.

The implication, however, was that the B-2 production rate would start to rise from the first year of production: two aircraft delivered in the first year, four more the year after that, in an accelerating stream until, in the last two years of production, Northrop would build thirty B-2s a year. From an industrial viewpoint, it was close to ideal.

No matter how Northrop and the USAF tried to present the plan, and no matter how much testing had been done in wind tunnels and simulators before AV-1 even rolled out, it seemed too risky for Congress to accept. One of the main reasons was the unfortunate history of the B-1B.

The task of producing the B-1 airframe, engines, and most of the avionics was completed on time and under budget. This achievement was much more than overshadowed by the problems with the Eaton-AIL ALQ-161 electronic warfare (EW) system. In the original, pre-Carter B-1A program, the ALQ-161 had been launched later than the rest of the system and was only in the early design stages when the production program was canceled. When it was restarted, the ALQ-161 was the only major element of the system that had not been tested thoroughly, but the accelerated schedule for deployment allowed little time for testing. It was never flown before it was installed in a B-1B; it had only been bench-tested, using simulated electronic signals rather than real devices. When it did fly, it proved to suffer from chronic, inherent technical problems; by 1988, two years after the problem surfaced, the USAF did not have a final plan for fixing the ALQ-161.

As a result, it became clear that Congress would not approve "concurrent" development and production of the B-2. The start of work on production of B-2s was delayed to take account of the late start of flight testing; it was further postponed so that more flight tests, including the first stage of observables testing, could be completed before production could begin.

By the time these decisions were taken, in 1988-89, preparations for production were well under way, and more than 40,000 people were working on the B-2 program. Simply suspending production would have had a catastrophic impact on the program; workers would have been lost, together with their hard-earned knowledge, and many subcontractors would have had to find other business. Instead, the entire program was stretched out, so that the USAF would buy only a handful of B-2s per year until the start of full-rate production could be authorized.

As well as indicating unhappiness with the Pentagon's planned starting date for the production program, Congress also objected to the pace of the effort. Representative Les Aspin, the Wisconsin Democrat who chaired the House Armed Services Committee, led a movement to reduce the peak rate: by mid-1989, it was clear that the thirty-per-year rate would never be reached.

The objections centered on the fact that the program's annual procurement cost would peak at $8 billion, at a time when the defense budget was declining. This would, undoubtedly, represent a large chunk of the total procurement budget for those years, but the Pentagon argued that it would be a once-only investment. Lawmakers, however, were obdurate, fearing that the B-2 would crowd out other needed programs, such as the C-17 transport. The full production rate would not be approved.

Delays and stretch-outs, of course, do not reduce the cost of any program; they increase it substantially. Because of the way that the costs of US military programs are calculated and expressed, moreover, the visible increase is larger than the actual rise in the program costs. A basic understanding of these numbers is essential to the B-2 debate.

"A billion here, a billion there, and pretty soon you're talking real money"— a line usually attributed to Sen. Everett Dirksen—has been a Washington joke for years. But the question of how to define "real money" is critical to public perception of the debate over defense spending, particularly in the United States.

Four factors form the bounds of the debate. First, inflation appears to be endemic. Second, military research, development, and production programs often last twenty to twenty-five years, so the inflation over that period makes a very big difference to the numbers. Third, the Pentagon uses several different methods of expressing procurement costs. Fourth, mass media commentators and politicians seldom qualify a cost figure by explaining its base.

Economic inflation is running at about 4 per cent per year. Year to year, the impact of this on people's lives is limited and it is politically acceptable. If compounded over twenty years, however, four per cent inflation will more than double any price or cost.

If long-term projects, military or civilian, were costed solely with inflated dollars, and the estimates were compared only with current money, it is unlikely that any venture spread over more than five years would get started. Before a program can start, its costs have to be put into perspective against the overall annual budget. This also provides a realistic, understandable yardstick to compare the costs of two different approaches to a requirement.

At the start of a program, therefore, the Pentagon quotes costs in "base-year" dollars. A base-year is usually the year before the program starts. The base-year cost is always described as such, and projected inflation rates are also contained in the Pentagon budget.

The other way of presenting costs is in the form of "then-year" dollars: each year's planned spending is increased according to the projected inflation rate.

Neither base-year nor then-year dollars are "real money." Base-year costs are less than today's dollars. Then-year costs are higher than today's dollars for the future years of the program, lower in the case of costs already sunk in the program.

Both are accounting tools and both have their uses. As the program progresses, though, the gap between base-year and current-year costs grows larger, and then-year costs—which are on average closer to the current year—are more realistic.

In the case of aircraft, the Pentagon also uses both "program" and "flyaway" costs. Program cost is made up of research, development, tooling, and production of all the aircraft in the program, all their subsystems, initial spares, and any support equipment (such as test equipment and simulators) specific to the type. Dividing the program cost by the number of aircraft to be built yields the "unit program cost."

Flyaway cost is the price of one aircraft and all its fixed equipment; research, development, tooling, and spares are not included. Once production has started, flyaway cost is usually quoted in then-year dollars. Discounting inflation, it declines during the production run because of learning-curve effects.

Both program and flyaway costs have their uses at different times. Program cost is the true measure of the resources required to fill a certain requirement and the baseline for controlling costs in the development stage. Program cost will tell you, for instance, whether it is worth spending more on research, development or tooling to reduce the flyaway cost. Once development is over, however, program cost is of purely historic significance, because the development money has been spent and cannot be recovered; flyaway cost determines how many aircraft can be afforded each year.

The highest cost that can be quoted for a single aircraft is a then-year unit program cost. When such numbers are quoted in the media, however, it is seldom explained that they are inflated beyond current-year values, the degree of which depends on the number of years left until the last aircraft is delivered.

Concentration on unit program costs also works against programs such as the B-2, which has pioneered a great deal of technology—manufacturing, mass-produced, low-observable structures, and "quiet" radar among them—on a relatively small production base. The B-2's non-recurring costs are almost a third of the program cost (one sixth is more typical) and, as a result, the unit program cost is high.

The abuse of the then-year unit program cost distorts debate over funding. Stretch-outs in production cause the real cost to rise, because lower manufacturing rates are less economical; they have a double impact on the then-year unit program cost, however, because they defer deliveries into later years with higher inflation.

The idea that the then-year unit program cost is the price of each aircraft gives rise to other distortions, because people naturally think that such a sum is "saved" every time one aircraft is eliminated from the program. This will, of course, save only the flyaway cost of the eliminated aircraft, and since it is, by definition, the last aircraft in the production run, even the flyaway cost is much lower than the average.

Eliminating the last, least expensive aircraft from the program has another effect: the unit program cost goes up, because the non-recurring costs are now divided by a smaller number of production aircraft.

In fact, most of the increases in the then-year unit program cost of the B-2 have resulted directly from Congressional action or pressure. When the program started, the total cost was estimated at $36.6 billion in 1981 dollars, a then-year unit program cost of $277 million. The cost increased, due to the 1983-84 wing redesign and other factors. By late 1988, real costs had increased by about 20 per cent, to $42.5 billion in 1981 dollars, leading to a then-year program cost of $68 billion. This estimate, however, was still based on concurrent development and the original high production rate, and even at that time, it was most unlikely that such a program would be approved.

During 1989, with the collapse of the Warsaw Pact, Congress pressed for further cuts in the defense budget, which, accounting for inflation, had been declining since 1985. Defense Secretary Richard Cheney ordered a review of the Pentagon's bigger new aircraft programs: the B-2, the US Navy's A-12 bomber, the Advanced Tactical Fighter, and the C-17 transport.

The purpose of the Major Aircraft Review (MAR) was to reduce expenditures while keeping intact the massive and long-term program to apply Stealth technology to most US military aviation missions. It also reflected the fact that the only way to achieve long-term savings in the defense budget was to reduce the size of the total force, which reduced the need for new aircraft.

The B-2, however, was in many ways the most vulnerable of the programs covered by the MAR, because its primary mission was directly linked to the military capability and intentions of the Soviet Union. As aggressive moves by the Soviet Union became less likely, and as economic problems within the Soviet bloc delayed and disrupted the modernization of Soviet air defenses, the need for the B-2 became less urgent.

Under the MAR, the total planned B-2 buy was cut from 132 to seventy-five aircraft, and the production rate was cut drastically: instead of a steady increase to a maximum of thirty-three aircraft in the final year, the rate would reach a plateau of twelve aircraft a year in the mid-nineties. Then-year program cost would decline from $75.4 billion (having increased since late 1988 due to the delay in production) to $61.1 billion.

A 19 per cent cost saving as a result of a 43 per cent cut in output may seem asymmetric, but it has to be remembered that the non-recurring costs of the program were unaffected by the cutback (most of them had been spent) and savings were further offset by the lower and less efficient production rate.

Unfortunately, and inevitably, the MAR cutbacks sent the B-2 then-year unit program cost zooming upwards, from $570 million to $815 million. Further delays increased the total program cost to $64.8 billion, or $864 million per aircraft by mid-1991. The latter figure was almost invariably used by the media and politicians in 1991-92. In the course of attempting to save money, the Pentagon has made the B-2—in the public's eye—much more expensive.

The root of this paradox is that the then-year unit program cost is a near-meaningless number which misleads much more than it informs. You cannot buy one B-2 for $864 million, or three for $2,592 million, because a bomber is not a washing machine or a car, bought from a showroom at a price determined by the market. The Pentagon does not buy one airplane at a time. It buys complete programs, from the awarding of the development contract to the retirement of the last aircraft, to give the armed services the equipment they need to perform the missions with which they are tasked.

Although the world has changed dramatically since the B-2 was conceived, the basic argument in favor of the program rests on the same principle: that the B-2 program is a more cost-effective way of covering the spectrum of necessary missions that it performs than any alternative aircraft or missile.

Moreover, the only realistic basis for this argument is future spending. Geopolitical shifts do not make it possible to recover the money already spent on the B-2. This irritates B-2 opponents, because each year's budget reduces the cost of completing the program, but the fact remains that "cost-to-complete" is the only valid measure by which solutions to military requirements may be compared. In 1991, cost-to-complete stood at

$34.8 billion for a seventy-five-aircraft force.

On this basis, the USAF concluded that two B-2 wings were a sensible use of its resources. At the same time, the USAF planned to draw down its force of tactical interdiction aircraft. In the mid-eighties, with the total fighter force at thirty-eight wings, the USAF had four wings of F-111s and planned another four wings of F-15Es. As the F-111s are retired in the early 2000s, they will be replaced one-for-one by a version of the Navy's A-12.

While the overall fighter force is now being cut to twenty-six wings (to be reached by 1995), the interdictors have taken a disproportionately heavy hit. Most of the F-111s are to be retired, the A-12 has been canceled, and only half the planned number of F-15Es is being bought. The twenty-six-wing force of the late nineties will have only two interdictor wings. The advent of the B-2 made these cuts palatable. It is by far the best conventional bomber ever designed, and its long range makes it quickly available to reinforce USAF strength in any theater.

With the demise of the A-12, the B-2 is the only new Stealth aircraft that can be operational before 2001, and the only new air-to-ground Stealth type that will be ready before 2005. Until then, if the B-2 does not go ahead, the US Stealth strike force will consist solely of F-117s. Even the currently planned upgrades will not allow the F-117s to hit its targets in adverse weather, and the F-117 carries only one-tenth of the B-2's weapon load.

Meanwhile, three B-2s are now flying. By late September 1991, they had completed 270 hours of flying. AV-1 had opened up the basic flight envelope and had conducted a first series of Stealth tests. AV-2, which made its first flight in September 1990, had done less flying than expected, because it had been grounded for modifications to the "deck" sections aft of the exhausts, which have experienced some cracking due to high temperatures and are being rebuilt using more advanced materials. AV-3 flew in June 1991, and has started tests of the radar. AV-4 and AV-5 should have joined the program by the time this book appears, and AV-6—the last full-scale development aircraft—is to fly before the end of 1992.

One B-2 airframe has already been tested to its ultimate design loads in a static test rig, housed in the Palmdale hangar where Lockheed used to build the TriStar airliner. Next door, another B-2 has already "flown" through a complete 10,000 hour life, with hydraulic jacks stretching and bending the structure to simulate flight loads. Based on a detailed analysis of SAC operations, the durability test even took account of the fact that SAC aircraft make more right turns than left turns on the ground. The first life—equivalent to twenty years—was completed in April 1991. Tear-down tests showed that problems were minimal and were confined to secondary structure and fasteners, and a second life test will start in the summer of 1992.

Most test results have been close to their predicted values. The only significant anomaly came in signature tests in July 1991, when a scheduled modification did not yield the reduction in RCS which had been predicted. The result was that RCS in one combination of aspect and waveband did not meet the specified value.

The problem is most likely to have involved the radar-absorbing structure (RAS) of the leading edge. The fact that Pentagon officials continued to stress that the RCS attained in the test was lower than that of the F-117 suggests strongly that the problem was in the low-frequency regime, where the B-2's size and ability to carry deep-section RAS give it an inherent advantage over smaller aircraft. Apparently, the problem was partly caused by a design change aimed at reducing costs, and the earlier design is available as a back up should other measures fail.

The pace of the test program has not been rapid; after more than two years, only 5 per cent of the planned test hours had been completed. At this stage, one observation can be made about the flight test program: it has not unearthed any problems that might have required any fundamental or major redesign of the aircraft, so it is still an open question whether Congress's ban on concurrency—a multi-billion-dollar insurance premium—was justified.

Northrop and Pentagon officials say that the program is still on track, and that tests will be completed by the time the USAF is ready to operate the aircraft. In part, the test program has been slow because the B-2 is a complex, new aircraft. The prototypes are also so heavily instrumented that each flight gathers a great deal of data, and there is little point in flying the aircraft again before the last flight's data have been analysed. At this point in the program, too, a B-2 flight is a complex operation; former USAF Systems Command chief Gen. Bernard Randolph has compared it to a Space Shuttle launch.

However, another reason for the pace of the test program is that there is no point whatsoever in completing the test effort before the USAF has enough aircraft to form a squadron. Because of the delays imposed on the program by Congress, AV-6 will not fly until 1992, even though it was ordered before 1987.

Ten production B-2s are now on order, having been authorized at a rate of two aircraft per year in fiscal years 1987 through 1991. This rate is absurdly low, but it was the only way to obey the Congressional ban on concurrency without completely halting the production line, which would have cost even more. The two-per-year rate sustains the workforce at a level that—with normal learning-curve effects—will support the higher rates planned at the end of the program.

The fiscal year 1987 aircraft will probably not be delivered until 1993. Even at the steady two-per-year rate permitted by the 1987-91 budgets, however, the B-2 is basically a "sixty-month airplane"; from the time that long-lead-time contracts are signed, it takes five years for a completed aircraft to roll off the line. Therefore, it will be 1996 before the USAF has enough aircraft to form a ten-aircraft bombardment squadron, and common sense dictates that the flight test program be paced so that it will be completed in that year. The B-2 will probably be declared operational in 1996 or 1997, some five years behind the original schedule. If it survives its political problems, it is likely to remain in service long after most of us have retired. But very few aircraft will be in service in any case. In January 1992, facing an election campaign on domestic issues, President Bush announced that only twenty operational B-2s would be completed—twenty-one aircraft, including AV-2. These will form two squadrons.

The decision was purely political. It has been taken in advance of any assessment or analysis of the future US force structure. As well as terminating the B-2, the administration backs the Navy's plan to develop a new long-range attack aircraft for the carriers, despite the limited role which they could play in the Gulf. Meanwhile, the argument that the B-2 can assume missions which are currently assigned to tactical air forces or carrier air groups has not been studied in any detail.

Predictably, in early 1992, the Democratic presidential challengers have promised more defense cuts than the administration, including the complete termination of the B-2 program. At this point, the savings will be relatively small; but the voters (who, thanks to the administration's latest cuts, can now read about the "$2 billion B-2") are persuaded otherwise.

More than half a century ago, the USAAF wanted to buy a new bomber. It was large, sophisticated, and the most expensive combat aircraft in the world.

Critics in Congress and the other branches of the military argued that economic times were tight and that the United States was not about to become embroiled in any conflicts where the big bomber's assets—range and survivability—would be necessary. A cheaper warplane, based on an existing airframe to save money, would be adequate.

The USAAF lost its fight and received only a small test squadron of the big bombers. Most of the money earmarked for bombers went to buy hundreds of the less-expensive aircraft.

The cheaper bomber was the Douglas B-18A Bolo, a derivative of the DC-2 airliner. In the Air Force Museum, a plaque in front of an immaculate B-18 sums up its front-line combat career: "Several of these aircraft were destroyed by the Japanese on December 7, 1941." The big, costly bomber that the nation could not afford was, of course, the Boeing B-17 Flying Fortress.

Appendices

B-2 Data

B-2 Data

Dimensions
Wingspan   172ft (52.4m)
Length   69ft (21m)

Weights
Operational, empty   155,000lb (70,300kg)
Fuel capacity   180,000lb (81,600kg)
Weapon load   50,000lb (22,700kg)
Maximum takeoff   385,000lb (174,600kg)

Performance
Cruising speed   Mach 0.85/560mph (900km/h) at 36,000 ft (11,000m)
Speed at sea level   Mach 0.8/610mph (980km/h)
Service ceiling   Above 50,000ft (15,000m)

Range

Weapons	Weight (lb)	Low-altitude segment (miles)	Unrefueled range (miles)
8 SRAM 8 B83	37,300 (16,900kg)	1,150 (1,850km)	5,070 (8,160km)
8 SRAM 8 B83	37,300 (16,900kg)	0	6,100 (9,800km)
8 SRAM 8 B61	24,000 (10,900kg)	1,150 (1,850km)	5,180 (8,340km)
80 Mk82	40,000 (18,140kg)	1,150 (1,850km)	5,550 (8,940km)

Index